Steeped in the Holy

Steeped in the Holy

Preaching as Spiritual Practice

Raewynne J. Whiteley

COWLEY PUBLICATIONS
Lanham · Chicago · New York · Toronto · Plymouth, UK

Published by Cowley Publications
An imprint of Rowman & Littlefield Publishers, Inc.
A wholly owned subsidiary of The Rowman & Littlefield Publishing Group, Inc.
4501 Forbes Boulevard, Suite 200, Lanham, Maryland 20706

Estover Road
Plymouth PL6 7PY
United Kingdom

Distributed by National Book Network

British Library Cataloguing in Publication Information Available

Library of Congress Cataloging-in-Publication Data

Whiteley, Raewynne J., 1966–
  Steeped in the holy : preaching as spiritual practice / Raewynne J. Whiteley.
     p. cm.
  ISBN-13: 978-1-56101-318-0 (cloth : alk. paper)
  ISBN-10: 1-56101-318-8 (cloth : alk. paper)
  ISBN-13: 978-1-56101-301-2 (pbk. : alk. paper)
  ISBN-10: 1-56101-301-3 (pbk. : alk. paper)
  1. Preaching. I. Title.
  BV4211.3.W45 2008
  251—dc22   2007023149

Printed in the United States of America.

The Windows

Lord, how can man preach thy eternall word?
      He is a brittle crazie glasse:
Yet in thy temple thou dost him afford
      This glorious and transcendent place,
      To be a window, through thy grace.

But when thou dost anneal in glasse thy storie,
      Making thy life to shine within
The holy Preachers; then the light and glorie
      More rev'rend grows, and more doth win:
      Which else shows watrish, bleak, & thin.

Doctrine and life, colours and light, in one
      When they combine and mingle, bring
A strong regard and aw: but speech alone
      Doth vanish like a flaring thing,
      And in the eare, not conscience ring.

George Herbert, *The Temple* (1633)

for my parents, Sue and Andrew,
for introducing God to me

and
for Wendy and Jon,
for offering a place where my soul could flourish

Contents

Acknowledgments

$\mathcal{T}$his book began in a conversation with other Gen X clergy, when we admitted to one another the struggles we had in maintaining our spiritual lives in the midst of all the demands of ministry. As a result, I began to wonder what it would be like to reconceive one aspect of ministry, preaching, not as a discrete task in itself but as an expression of our ongoing relationship with God.

The chapter on sacrament, which is foundational for the rest of the book, comes out of my doctoral work in homiletics at Princeton Theological Seminary. I am grateful for the wisdom and friendship of my advisor, James Kay, and dissertation committee, Charles L. Bartow and Charles L. Rice (the latter of Drew University), and to the other faculty whose teaching finds its way into these pages.

I am thankful to the Cathedral College of Preachers, whose fellowship gave me time and space to begin the work of turning an academic work into something my peers might actually want to read, and for the friendships there that have enriched my life over the past twelve years and made it my home away from home here in the United States.

And, of course, probably most important are the people of the churches in which I have served and preached, particularly those of Trinity Church in Princeton, the Episcopal Church at Princeton University, Trinity Cathedral in Trenton, and Trinity "Old Swedes" Church in Swedesboro. They have listened patiently, offered advice and encouragement, shared my passion for preaching, and, most of all, found God at work in their own lives and been willing to share that experience.

A Designated God Person

$\mathcal{R}$ecently Sam, aged four, returned to our parish for his baby sister's baptism. The family had moved away from the area, so I hadn't seen him for a few months. As he came up the sidewalk and caught sight of me, he said excitedly to his mother, "There's Jesus!"

I am not Jesus, and I have no illusions that I might be. As I explained to Sam's mother, it's just a stage many children go through. The priest stands up in the front of the church and talks about God; the priest takes bread and wine and echoes the words of Christ, "This is my body; this is my blood." No wonder small children identify the priest with Christ. And it's not just children. When I returned to my former government job for the summer after my first year of seminary, I found myself being referred to as the "God person."

It's not so much confusion, as a recognition that this person is in *imitatio Christi*, re-presenting Christ, re-presenting Christ to the gathered community called by his name. We act as intermediaries, interpreters, by the grace of the Holy Spirit—not because ordinary Christians can't come to God directly, but because sometimes they need midwives, guides, people willing to stand beside them before the dangerous passion of God. And sometimes God needs us to embody the gospel, because human beings sometimes do better at hearing the word of God in flesh and blood rather than ink. We need a designated God person.

That places a heavy burden on clergy. We know all too well that we are not any more holy than anyone else. We live in the same world, a world of constant demands and crazy schedules. Aside from the usual pressures of family life, our work time is largely unstructured. We can make plans, but all too often get distracted by other things. A parishioner needs to get into the church to measure the space for a bench he is building. Someone calls to see if I know if there will be a historical house tour in town. A parishioner dies, and we have a funeral and lunch. The treasurer wants to drop by with my paycheck. Someone else calls about a newspaper article and leaves a message that needs to be answered in the next twelve hours, and so I have to hunt down the volunteer who knows the answer. And the monthly newsletter still isn't finished. The nice quiet day I had set aside for prayer and reflection and getting a start on my sermon is gone. It's all part of our calling—the conversations with parishioners, interactions with the local community, administration, and funerals, along with sermon preparation and prayer. But sometimes we get swamped by the things that need immediate attention; it can feel like we are losing our connection with the Holy.

As I have reflected on this, it strikes me that one of the problems is that we tend to view our own spiritual lives as somehow separate from our ministry. One is something we do for ourselves; the other, something we do for the church. But it's a false division. They are integrally connected. Without a life lived in an active relationship with God, our souls shrivel and our ministries suffer. Our life of faith is essential for us to be who we are called to be: God people. We can't fake it. We need to be connected into the life of God.

The aim of this book is to explore one area of Christian ministry, preaching, as it is integrally related to the life and practices of the soul. Most of us came to the practice of preaching through seminary. We always knew that we would have to preach some time, but often our first taste was in a classroom, in the context of an academic degree. It's hard to break the idea that we're doing this for credit, that this is an exercise of the mind. But in fact, it's an exercise of the spirit, of the soul. And to preach effectively, we need to prepare our souls, to have them in a state of readiness for the Spirit of God to use us as conduits of grace. Thomas Moore offers a wonderful description of how this can work: "By caring for the soul faithfully, every day, we step out of the way and let our full genius emerge. Soul coalesces into the mysterious philosopher's stone, that rich, solid core of personality the alchemists sought, or it opens into the peacock's tail—a revelation of the soul's colors and a display of its dappled brilliance."[1] Caring for our souls will have rich rewards in our calling.

I have to admit a personal bias here. Preaching is, and always has been—since I preached my first sermon at the age of nineteen—the focus of my spiritual life. It is the place where I most clearly experience the Holy working in and through me, where I am most fully human, where I know the radically liberating grace of God. For me, the deepest prayer happens around the preparation and act of preaching

In the chapters that follow, I will explore how preaching is related to and indeed dependent on the spiritual practices related to sacrament, Scripture, hospitality, play, prayer, and embodiment. Each practice, while valuable in itself in cultivating our relationship with God, is also connected in fundamental ways with what we are doing as we preach. A vibrant, rich, and deep saturation in God prepares the way for us to speak about and on behalf of God; far from being a burden, our encounter with the Holy One can infuse our preaching—and our hearers—with life.

NOTE

1. Thomas Moore, *Care of the Soul: A Guide for Cultivating Depth and Sacredness in Everyday Life* (New York: HarperCollins, 1992), 305.

· 2 ·

Food for the Soul: Sacrament

*E*very three months or so, one of my friends heads to a specialty food store and buys a one-ounce jar of American Paddlefish caviar, a seven-ounce tin of salmon roe, four ounces of Scottish smoked salmon, crème fraîche, a baguette, and a bottle of Russian vodka. The three of us then gather for an evening of indulgence. It tastes wonderful.

But French bread and fish eggs go only so far. Our bodies need more nourishment, a greater variety, more substance. A quick snack, whether hamburgers or caviar, is not good enough to grow, strengthen, and sustain our bodies. We need the whole food pyramid—protein, carbohydrates, and even fat—to be healthy human beings.

Our souls are no different. They need feeding, strengthening, sustaining. However, the food of the soul is not protein, carbohydrates, and fat, but our spiritual practices. A central form of nourishment for our souls has always been the sacrament of the Eucharist. The physical eating of bread and wine is an easy analogue to the spiritual eating of Christ's body and blood. But if we listen to the wisdom of our forebears, we discover that the Eucharist is not the only place where we are nourished. Preaching, too, is food for our souls, nourishment that like the Eucharist provides sustenance for the spirit.

On the night before Jesus died, he took bread, blessed it, broke it, and shared it with his disciples. Then he took the cup, blessed it, and again shared it with his disciples. This meal is at the core of our Christian practice, the focus of our community week by week. Here, as we meet together around a table, we expect to meet with Christ.

We sometimes forget, however, that this first meal did not happen in holy isolation. Betrayal and death were looming over the disciples.

Jesus needed to teach them what they needed to know to sustain them in the difficult hours and weeks and years ahead. Love one another. Don't scramble for privilege. Offer gracious service. Pray.

We have the truths of that evening distilled for us, mostly in the Gospel of John. But it is clear, from John's account, that as they sat in that upper room that joyous, threatening evening, Jesus didn't just lob a few pithy sayings over a loaf of bread and cup of wine. This was a conversation, a teasing, struggling, heart-rending dialogue between Jesus and his friends, to prepare them to live out the gospel that he had lived and would die.

Three days later, there was another conversation, once again over bread and wine. Jesus opened the Scriptures to the disciples, making connections between the God of the pages and the God they had met, inflaming their hearts and inspiring—breathing new life—into their lives.

Word and sacrament embrace the defining event of our faith. Is it any wonder, then, that when Archbishop Cranmer worked on reforming the liturgy for the English church, he built a liturgical structure around the two, linking them in a central balanced, complementary relationship for the life of the church? He was simply reclaiming the tradition of Jesus's last, and first, nights with his friends.

They belong together, the word in speech and Word in sacrament. Through them, we are brought to saving faith and the benefits of Christ's death are brought to us; together they nourish the Christian life.

Since the liturgical movement of the early to mid-twentieth century, we have reclaimed the Eucharist as food for the soul; now it is time to likewise reclaim preaching. The sixteenth-century preacher Hugh Latimer went so far as to say, "Take away preaching, take away salvation"![1] Preaching is more than just teaching, more than just speaking theology well or clearly explicating Scripture. It is bringing the Word of God to life in the people of God.

But preaching does not, cannot, happen in isolation. Just as Jesus spoke with his friends in the context of those meals, so we speak in the context of a meal. That context, that meal, can bring richness and depth to our speech, reshaping how we understand ourselves and God to be at work in this holy event.[2]

NOURISHED IN THE WORD OF GOD

It doesn't take a great leap of the imagination to understand the bread and wine of the Eucharist as food for the soul: As we eat the bread and wine, we spiritually feed on Christ. The idea of preaching as food for the soul is a little harder to manage—we don't usually think of nourishment as being something that comes through our ears.

However, this association has a rich tradition in both Scripture and liturgical history. In the book of Hebrews, teaching (a word often used interchangeably with preaching) is described using the metaphor of milk and solid food. Beginning Christians need to be suckled with the milk of basic teaching; those who are more mature should be ready for solid food:

> For though by this time you ought to be teachers, you need someone to teach you again the basic elements of the oracles of God. You need milk, not solid food, for everyone who lives on milk, being still an infant, is unskilled in the word of righteousness. But solid food is for the mature, for those whose faculties have been trained by practice to distinguish good from evil. (Heb. 5:12–14; see also 1 Pet. 2:2–3; 1 Cor. 3:1–2a)

We Christians need to be fed, sometimes by milk, sometimes by solid food, and that feeding happens through preaching and teaching.

Of course this metaphor of nourishment has its origins much earlier. In Isaiah 55:1–3a, images of eating and of listening to the voice of God are interwoven:

> Ho, everyone who thirsts, come to the waters;
> and you that have no money, come, buy and eat!
> Come, buy wine and milk without money and without price.
> Why do you spend your money for that which is not bread,
> and your labor for that which does not satisfy?
> Listen carefully to me, and eat what is good,
> and delight yourselves in rich food.
> Incline your ear, and come to me;
> listen, so that you may live.

What is eaten is life-giving for the body; what is heard is life-giving for the soul. In the book of the prophet Ezekiel, the metaphor is even more graphic. The prophet is given a scroll for food; on it is written the divine message. The prophet is called on to literally eat the word of God, and speak it "from his belly": the eating is his preparation for preaching (Ezek. 3:1–3). It is an image that is echoed in the Psalms (19:10; 119:103), in Proverbs (16:24 and 24:3), and in Revelation 10:10—and the food is unexpectedly sweet. In Jeremiah 15:16, the divine words that the prophet eats become the delight of his heart.

Back in the New Testament, Jesus replies to the devil's scornful challenge, "If you are the Son of God, command this stone to become a loaf of bread," with a reminder that we do not live by bread alone, drawing on Deuteronomy 8:3: "He humbled you by letting you hunger, then by feeding you with manna, with which neither you nor your ancestors were acquainted, in order to make you understand that one does not live by bread alone, but by every word that comes from the mouth of the Lord." Bread is more than simply food in the mouth of Jesus. He himself is the bread of life. That bread of life can be eaten in the Eucharist. However, time after time in the gospels, it is Jesus's words that draw people into eternal life: They offer nourishment from the bread of life. Both the divine body and the divine word are food for the soul: Jesus Christ, body and word, is the complete food for those who believe in him.

Of course this comes as no surprise to those of us who have prayed the Lord's Prayer for a lifetime. "Give us today our daily bread." Taken literally, it is a prayer of trust in the God who provides for our physical needs. Taken metaphorically, it is a prayer of equal trust in the God who provides for our spiritual needs, feeding, nourishing, sustaining us.

MEAT, NOT STRAWBERRIES

This metaphor can enrich our preaching in two areas: form and content. The movement that introduced narrative preaching in the 1960s and 1970s was a wonderful gift to those who have to listen to sermons. After years of often dull-as-dishwater lectures, usually squeezed into a predictable three points, we began to hear of preaching that sounded like people actually believed it, that suggested that the Christian life might indeed be something of beauty and joy! But it has also been dangerous. Sometimes—too often—the beauty of lyrical storytelling has swallowed up the substance of the gospel. Content has been subjugated to form, and we come away feeling as though we have eaten a cream puff or an ice sculpture—beautiful to our senses, but leaving our stomachs and souls empty.

A nourishing sermon, on the other hand, is something which meets the deep hunger of the listeners. Lucy Lind Hogan puts it this way:

> As preachers we have the marvelous joy and privilege of spreading before our listeners the wonderful banquet of the Word of God, the message of [God's] love and graciousness. Whether it is the milk of our gospel message that "Christ has died, Christ has risen, Christ will come again" or the solid food of the call to give up all that we have, pick up our cross, and follow Jesus, we never lack for nourishing fare.[3]

To preach a nourishing sermon, we as preachers have to engage in substantial biblical, theological, cultural, and pastoral reflection in preparation, so that we can engage hearers at every level of their beings. There are no shortcuts. It's not enough to use preaching aids and glean the leftovers of other preachers' hard work. We need to take the time to pray, reflect, study, play—all the things that this book talks about—and then come to the pulpit ready to probe the struggles and ambiguities of life, so that our hearers leave church with something "to chew on," to sustain them in their lives day to day.

It's tempting to shy away from depth in sermons, especially in a culture that is apparently more interested in entertainment than sustenance. The entertainment paradigm for worship is attractive because it draws people in, but what they are drawn in for? Is it for entertainment, or worship? To observe, or to participate? If the primary purpose of our gathering together is to worship, to glorify God, then "easy listening" religion is a travesty. If our calling is to build up the people of God, a community of committed, faithful disciples, creating an "audience" culture will undermine the heart of our work. Preaching must have depth in order to sustain.

But if preaching is truly food for the soul, then there is work to be done by the listeners as well. When we eat a meal, we taste, we savor, we chew, we swallow, we digest—and we live on the basis of that nourishment. Those who eat are active participants in the meal.

Likewise, those who feed on the metaphorical food of preaching are also active participants. They must listen to the sermon carefully, opening their minds and hearts to the word of God, and taking time to reflect on it—the conscious tasting, chewing, and swallowing of the sermonic food. Early Benedictine monks took this seriously, reciting Scripture as they worked. They were sometimes known as the "munchers," chewing on Scripture as if on cud.

Then there is the unconscious act of digestion. This happens when listeners go about their daily lives, as the Holy Spirit works in cooperation with them to integrate the preached word into their life. Conscious and unconscious, human and Holy Spirit, work together to take the sermon from the church pew into everyday life.

If preaching is food for the soul, it needs to be frequent. Hugh Latimer, with his typically pithy language, put it this way: "Scripture calleth [the preaching of the word of God] meat; not strawberries, that come but once a year, and tarry not long, but are soon gone: but it is meat, it is no dainties. The people must have meat that must be familiar and continual, and daily given unto them to feed upon."[4] In Latimer's ideal world, there would be a sermon at every service, every day of the week, and certainly every time the Eucharist is celebrated. This is not snack food, not an optional, albeit flavorful, extra. This is the stuff that sustains life. Today most of us assume that sermons should be weekly events; however, sometimes we are tempted to allow them to be displaced by "special events" or shortened to make way for other parts of the service. But preaching is indispensable: It is "everyday nourishment" for the soul.

GRACED CREATION

But the wisdom of sacramental theology cannot be confined to the metaphor of food for the soul. Sacraments are, by definition, means of grace. "Outward and visible signs of inward and spiritual grace, given by Christ as sure and certain means by which we receive that grace" is how *The Book of Common Prayer* puts it.[5] In other words, while sacraments may be ordinary, tangible, earthly things, by some strange quirk of God's fancy they are at the same time reliable ways through which God reaches out to us.

Anyone who has taken time to reflect upon the world around him or her and to look for signs of God at work knows that divine grace can not be confined within the official sacraments. God's grace is so lavish that it appears all over the place, even when it is most unexpected. So we should not be surprised if we find God's grace at work in preaching. It might not have been traditionally counted as one of the sacraments, but all the same, it has frequently been recognized sacramental in nature, insofar as it functions as a means of grace.

One Reformation-period definition of the sacraments defines them as those things through which "[God] doth work invisibly in us, and doth not only quicken, but also strengthen and confirm our Faith in him."[6] Sacraments are not just vehicles or instruments through which God ministers grace, but are "sure and certain means." That is, God can reliably be encountered through them, and we can expect to receive the grace of Christ in his death and resurrection. We pay attention through them to God, and find ourselves in a relationship of grace.

The reliability of sacraments as a means of grace is rooted in the presence of Christ. By being incarnate, Christ has become a model for divine grace that is mediated to humanity though earthly, material, historical realities. The theologian John Macquarrie explores the relationship between divine grace and earthly, material realities in this way:

> [The Eucharist] makes use of outward, visible elements, in this case, bread and wine. It enshrines as its core and inner meaning a making-present of Christ and his grace. It incorporates the recipient into the body of Christ and conforms his existence to the pattern of Christ. All this and more is included in the Eucharist, and exemplifies the character of the sacraments generally.[7]

God communicates godself to us by the real, tangible everyday things that are part of our everyday life—we meet God in them. That is the sacramental principle.

So does all matter, by the nature of its essence and association with Christ, always communicate God to us? Not quite. All matter has the potential to function sacramentally, but it does not necessarily do so. The Archbishop of Canterbury, Rowan Williams, offers a useful clarification at this point, lest we overidentify the elements with Christ's presence:

> What makes sacraments distinct is what they are for, the activity in which they are caught up, which is making human beings holy. To put it another way, what makes the Christian sacraments unique is not so much something inherent in them, some "specialness" in the action, but the uniqueness of Jesus Christ in his dying and rising.[8]

It is God's peculiar choice that makes the sacraments efficacious as means of grace and mediators of Christ's presence, not any character of the elements, not the simple fact of being earthly matter.

What makes God choose some things and not others to function sacramentally is something we cannot know. Nor is it entirely clear exactly how it is that sacraments function as a means of grace. But they do. We know it because we have experienced it—the wonderful encounter with the divine through the everyday things of our lives. We meet God in them, and receive God's grace.

There are sacraments—numbering two or seven, depending on your tradition—and then there are things that function sacramentally. These are things that the church may not formally have identified as sacraments, but that we recognize as being potential vehicles of God's grace. Preaching is one such thing, with the potential to function sacramentally, though it cannot be guaranteed. In some traditions, preaching is primarily understood as teaching. Teaching people about their faith is important; however, that purpose is to do with the transfer of information, rather than the experience of grace. Other traditions barely nod to the preaching event, offering a brief personal reflection that is simply a prelude to the main event of the Eucharist. In neither case is there any expectation of God's involvement.

But if we follow Latimer's lead, preaching that functions as a means of grace provokes and strengthens faith. Perhaps he overstated it with his polemical claim, "Take away preaching; take away salvation." Yet his passion points to something important. Preaching *can* be a means by which we experience the presence of Christ the Word, and receive God's grace. If the sacraments are a visible sign of God's invisible grace, then preaching might be thought to be an audible sign of an inaudible grace. The Eucharist is grace through our eyes and mouths; preaching is grace through our ears. They catch us up in the reality and presence of Christ. Sacrament and word together evoke faith and effect grace, vehicles of God's promise.

If preaching functions as a means of grace, human words—human actions—become the vehicle of divine presence. God uses them to communicate godself to us with a directness and intensity that evokes and echoes that of the incarnation itself.

> Whether within the biblical text or beyond, words can and do thus function sacramentally, despite all their apparent clash and dissonance. For it is precisely through meditation upon such images that our participation in the Word made flesh is most effectively deepened. Chewing the Eucharistic elements and chewing the words should thus not be seen as opposed activities. Words, no less than the Word himself, can be fully sacramental. The divine Poet whose Word shaped the language of creation also thereby made possible the words—the human poetry—that describe that creation, and it is these words that enable us to participate in the Word as their source and ours.[9]

Preaching nourishes in us the faith, which, as the gift of God, enables us to claim the promises of God. It doesn't just invite us into the presence of God, but is the locus of God's presence among us. It enables us to participate in Christ. The preached word, like the sacraments, is a God-given means of grace. Here God makes God's own self known and brings us to a faith wherein we can know God's presence.

There is a practical dimension to this. Recent work on the theory of multiple intelligences has shown how differently different people's minds work. They respond to different stimuli; they think in different ways. Our traditional sacraments work well for those who receive and assimilate information visually and through the sense of taste and touch; preaching can reach those whose primary way of experiencing the world is auditory: They hear the grace of God.

So language becomes a vehicle of grace. The Word incarnate is present to us in words of faith. Preaching is sacramental, a place where we meet our Savior.

HUMAN WORDS, GOD'S WORDS

If preaching is a place where we meet Christ, then we must imagine that God is somehow present in this act. As a preacher, I tend to forget—or perhaps to ignore—this reality. There is a part of me that would prefer that God were out of the picture, safely removed so that I can get on with my work without that looming presence looking over my shoulder. But of course the alternative—that God might be absent—is even worse. Brought up to know that God is ever present, ever creating, to contemplate a world absent of God is to contemplate a world grinding to a halt. God *must* be here.

It's probably a no-brainer to say that God is at the very center of the homiletical task. Christ's words and actions give preaching its warrant. Christ is himself a model for preaching as a pastoral and prophetic task, and Christ himself forms the substance of preaching. We preach because Christ preached, and we preach Christ.

That sounds good in theory. But in practice, how do we preach Christ? How do we ensure that God is at the center of our preaching?

Some preachers answer this by being careful to make sure they name Jesus in every sermon, regardless of whether he is the focus or not. Others limit their preaching to the Gospels. The result is a tendency either to "find" Jesus in every text, whether merited or not—so the Ten Commandments become about Jesus, as does the story about David and Bathsheba and the more nihilistic wailings of Ecclesiastes—or the total ignoring of most of the Epistles (except where they explicitly talk about Jesus) and the Old Testament. Neither solution does justice to a robust theology of Scripture, which understands all Scripture as a vehicle through which God addresses us in some way or another.

Being true to the presence of Christ doesn't have to mean that we are limited to focusing on the words and actions of Jesus alone, that we must confine ourselves to preaching on the four Gospels, or that we must insert Jesus's name into every sermon "just to make sure." Rather, what we are called to do is to make the gospel, the good news of Jesus Christ, the criterion against which all preaching is judged.

In practical terms what that means is constantly holding our words up against what we know of Christ, asking ourselves, is this consistent with the good news he brought? So when we preach on the Ten Commandments, rather than jumping straight to Jesus's summary of the two greatest commandments or arguing that they have been superseded by grace, we might explore what the covenant that they encapsulate means in the light of grace. We might imagine them as a kind of honor code that safeguards relationships, rather than law code that demands punishment for failure. It's not that we should ban Jesus from the conversation, but that we consider each text in its own right and listen to what God and it are saying to us, rather than superimposing an artificial "word from our sponsor Jesus." As we do this, we will surely find God firmly in the center of our preaching.

But let's take this idea of God's presence in our preaching a little further. Many preachers are rightly wary of a literalistic approach that attributes to God all words spoken from the pulpit. Stuck in our minds are the stereotypes of fire-and-brimstone or ethical puritanicalism coming from fundamentalism, and papal infallibility coming from Roman Catholicism, where the sermon—and the preacher—are out-of-bounds for question or challenge. We don't want anything to do with these claims of God's presence. So we run for cover, settling for the safety of sermons that are individual reflections on Scripture and the life of faith, with input from God neither anticipated nor wanted. Preaching is just one beggar offering bread to another—a laudable but essentially power-abrogating undertaking.

However, if we take the risk and say, yes, God is present in the preached word, then we have to struggle with how it is that God speaks in and through human words. Because there is no doubt that these are human words: We work hard at finding them and putting them together. Anyone who has agonized over what to say on a Sunday morning knows that the preacher is more than a living dictation machine. But we also know that in some sense they are God's words. No amount of hard work or skill can account for those occasions—and there are surprisingly many of them—when a profound silence falls over the congregation and we hear something beyond the words, something unequivocally holy.

We tend to assume that words can only be one thing or another, God's voice or a human voice. It's part of that human tendency to try to draw boundaries, to separate things into compartments, to define everything with a level of precision drawn from our love affair with science. But as any physicist will tell you, it's not always possible to do that. Things in this world of ours are notoriously hard to grasp hold of. And when you add in the otherworldly, it gets even more difficult to tie down.

In a normal conversation, it is easy to determine who is speaking when. In literature, it's a little more difficult to assign text to different writers, though we seem to have managed quite well in the field of Bible studies by attributing authorship with the help of source critical theory or by apportioning bits of Isaiah.

When it comes to working out whether preaching is God's voice or a human voice, or some sort of combination of the two, however, it becomes somewhat more difficult. Textual criticism doesn't really help, not least because we're the ones putting these words together and it's too late to wait until after the sermon is delivered to decide if God made it in or not!

It is here that we return to our sacramental idea of preaching. Sacramental theology provides us with a model for this dual presence. The presence of Christ in the Eucharist and the presence of God in preaching can be understood as being in parallel. In the Eucharist, the bread and wine are received physically and Christ received spiritually. In preaching, the words of the preacher are heard physically and the word of God received spiritually. The preacher becomes the instrument of God's presence. The divine doesn't displace the human, but works in and through it.

There is, of course, a risk in taking seriously the idea that the sermon is a place where God is present. It means we are not alone in the preaching enterprise. On days when the words flow like treacle, this may be a comfort—if I fail, surely God will come through for me. But at 5:30 on Sunday morning, the internal script is more likely to go something like this: "I've spent all week on this. I just don't know how to begin. I'm a failure. God must hate me. I'm going to get up there and everyone will know that I'm a fraud. I should resign, leave this ministry, go get a real job."

Usually, in my experience, God does come through. But the fear is still there: What if I fail God? What if God wants to be present, and I mess up?

Then there is the opposite temptation. On the rare occasion that I preach a killer sermon, the kind where every word drops into an electric silence, I am tempted to attribute it all to my hard work. Why should God claim any credit? It was my hard work, hour after hour, that created this thing.

At the heart of this is the question of to what extent we are responsible for what we say. If we say that God is present, perhaps our hard work in preparing the sermon is of negligible value.

Once again, sacramental theology provides us with a model for how this human-divine interaction occurs. The same tension exists in the Eucharist, as we struggle with how bread and wine, the work of human hands, become for us the body and blood of our Lord, the means of our salvation.

The traditional answer to this has been epiclesis, literally "calling down." The Holy Spirit is invoked on the elements, so that the bread and wine both become the body and blood of Christ to us and remain bread and wine, in order that those who share in the elements may receive the blessings or benefits of salvation. Likewise in preaching, it is through the Holy Spirit, who enlivens and inspires us, that the preached word can be both human word and the word of God. God is present not only in the words spoken, but in the whole process leading up to preaching and, indeed, in the response of the people.

The grace of this epiclesis is well captured in the following hymn by Charles Wesley:

> Come, thou everlasting Spirit,
> Bring to every thankful mind
> All the Saviour's dying merit,
> All his sufferings for mankind!
> True Recorder of his passion,
> Now the living faith impart;
> Now reveal his great salvation;
> Preach his gospel to our heart.
>
> Come, thou Witness of his dying;
> Come, Remembrancer Divine!
> Let us feel thy power, applying
> Christ to every soul, — and mine!
> Let us groan thine inward groaning;
> Look on him we pierced, and grieve;
> All receive the grace atoning,
> All the sprinkled blood receive.[10]

If, through the Holy Spirit, God is present in our preaching, it is humbling and encouraging and fearful at the same time. We cannot take this task lightly—it behooves our attentiveness, as to God, an act of obedience and service. Yet the final weight of responsibility does not rest on us alone, but on the God who created us and our language, and whose Holy Spirit works within us.

So how is it that God actually works in the sermon? If preaching is a means of grace, how does it work? What is the connection between God's work in the past—particularly in the life, death, and resurrection of Christ—and God's action in the present? How is our testimony to God's past action related to our experience of God in the context of our life of faith today?

Some preachers see the primary purpose of preaching as being (solely) to testify to the completed acts of God as they are recorded in Scripture. It's essentially exegesis from the pulpit. Preaching like this inevitably becomes indistinguishable from teaching, a purely pedagogical approach.

Other preachers continue to acknowledge Scripture as a temporally bounded record of God's past actions and speech. However, God also acts in parallel in the present, speaking to us spiritually in the preaching event. So on the one hand we have the story, and on the other we look for equivalent situations in our lives. We learn from the example of the saints. Scripture becomes a source for moral theology, a guide for the present. But God doesn't really come into the picture.

But there is a third way. Here preaching takes seriously God's involvement in and through the preaching event. In the sermon, God addresses the people of God and draws them to faith; God's being and acts as evidenced in Scripture are appropriated in the present through the power of the Holy Spirit.

Eucharistic theology provides us with the language for this way of understanding preaching: anamnesis, "that lively contact with the past that appropriates its effects in the present."[11] The concept of anamnesis comes from the words of Christ at the Last Supper:

$$\text{τοῦτο ποιεῖτε εἰς τὴν ἐμὴν ἀνάμνησιν}$$

commonly translated "do this in remembrance of me" (1 Cor. 11:24; Luke 22:19). This remembrance, anamnesis, carries with it the overtones of the Hebrew root, וכר, an act of remembering that is inseparable from action. And so the anamnesis of the Eucharist is to encounter the crucified and risen Christ, to experience the effects of his actions here and now. It is not simply a matter of human remembering, but of God's activity, not only in the past events which are the subject of recollection, but also in the present encounter between God and humanity. In the eucharistic anamnesis, past, present, and future, heavenly and earthly action, coalesce into one unified event-experience. Eternity touches history.

If preaching is about anamnesis, we not only remember the past acts of God, but enter into their reality across time and taste the eschatological future in the present. Past, present, and future are fused together.

But this does not mean a total obliteration of time. Anamnesis in preaching does not mean returning to a precritical perspective where Scripture is interpreted as God's direct and present word to us, without any hermeneutical gap. Instead, we find that the connection between God's work recounted in Scripture and God's work in our world today is the eternal One who touches both points and brings them into relationship.

In preaching as anamnesis, our world—both in the time of Scripture and today—is embraced by God's world. Time telescopes: We are invited to rediscover our reality in the midst of God's reality, our world in the midst of God's world.

French bread and fish eggs or steak and potatoes? Preaching that is food for the soul is both. It is rich and deep, infused with the presence and grace of God.

Empty Hands
A Sermon

I can still remember the feel of summer vacations when I was a kid.

There were those first delicious days of anticipation where it seemed that anything was possible, the first trip to the beach, a sleepover, and the promise of a visit with my grandparents. Time seemed endless, and life was wonderful.

But as the weeks wore on, the signs of the end increasingly encroached on my summer. There was the inevitable trip to the mall for new shoes—not much time left for bare feet—pencils to be labeled, and three months' worth of piano practice to be done.

Summer is just three months of the year, but in those three months we have a microcosm of our lives at large.

As children, our lives stretch before us. We play at being firefighters and soldiers and teachers, we imagine ourselves as ballerinas and astronauts, and our lives are full of possibility and adventure.

But as we grow older, it's all too clear that the end of the summer is not so far away. Our dreams lose their glistening feathers and fall to the ground and get trampled under our own feet. We must be sensible and prudent and prepare for our retirement. Our bodies begin to creak and groan—the first gray hairs, the aches that might just be the beginnings of arthritis, and a simple tiredness that seems to come from nowhere. And the world around us, and the ideal life presented on TV, becomes further and further from the secure reality we once knew.

The end of the summer: Our bodies betray us, our choices condemn us, our world bears down on us. Death and life become muddled together.

And then we hear Jesus, and he seems to be just as caught up in the muddle as we are.

"I am the bread of life, the bread come down from heaven," he says. "Whoever eats of this bread will never die; whoever believes has eternal life."

And the people around him stare, and some laugh, because they know his father and his mother, know that this is no heavenly apparition but just young Jesus bar Joseph, son of a carpenter, vagabond, and storyteller. And for all that he made a feast for five thousand from a few loaves and fishes, they will all be hungry again, and he will be too, and they will all die, whether from famine or illness, in a skirmish with the occupying troops, or, if God is gracious, as righteous elders at home in their beds.

We all know that death will eventually come. We can prolong our lives with healthy lifestyles and good medical care; we can fight against the diseases and the violence that ravish our world, but in the end we will all die, and there's no way of avoiding it.

And these claims of Jesus of eternal life are as muddled as anything else. Because on the one hand there is a security about it, the idea that death isn't the end of everything, that the people we love are safely waiting somewhere, looking forward to a joyous reunion, but on the other there is always the fear that comes from the skepticism of our world that we're just kidding ourselves. That this heaven thing is about as unreal as those little round-eyed children on the Precious Moments cards, and we'd better get on with life in the grainy reality of the here and now.

We can just about deal with Easter and the resurrection, as long as it's only Jesus, but when it comes to us, it's a whole 'nother story. Because heaven, and life eternal with it, has got a bad name.

We're embarrassed, most of us, by those people who walk the streets demanding of strangers: "Have you been washed in the blood of the lamb?" Who knock on our doors saying: "If you were to die tonight, what would you say at the gates of heaven?"

It smacks of the pious righteousness which we all too often associate with a joyless fanatical religion, one in which we are expected to leave our brains outside the church doors.

And so, it seems to me, in response, sometimes we go to the other extreme. We avoid talking about heaven or anything which could possibly be construed as otherworldly, and we focus our attention on the world around us. Instead of focusing on some ethereal kingdom of God after death, we focus on bringing about that kingdom of God in the here and now. We might not use those words for it, but that's what we're doing as we seek transformation in our own lives, and as we work to bring that transformation into other people's lives as well. And so we get active in the local community, with Motel Meals and Crisis Ministry, the Trenton After School Program and Done in a Day. And that's certainly part of the Christian gospel. But it's not the whole of it.

Because there's no getting around it—what Jesus is talking about in today's Gospel is about life and death and life after death.

Part of the problem is that there are no real details about what this life after death will be like. We get glimpses throughout the New Testament—transformed bodies, no more tears, some sort of closeness to God—but nothing really tangible, nothing we can grasp hold of with the kind of certainty we'd like, certainly nothing that could be considered as proof. Of course, there's Jesus's resurrection, but even that doesn't tell us a whole lot more.

But I want to say that today's reading fills in just a little bit of that picture; and it does it in a way that maybe, just maybe, begins to make a connection between the kingdom of God in heaven and the kingdom of God here on earth, between eternal life after death and eternal life which is now.

Jesus talks of himself as the bread of life. Eating this bread, whatever that means, eternal life. And bread is on his hearers' minds. The way John tells the story, Jesus speaks these words the day after he has fed the five thousand; those same people are here to hear him again, full of the bread they ate by the lakeside. This bread is as real and satisfying as the crumbs that lie heavily on their stomachs. And this bread is as real and as satisfying as the manna was in the desert, which if you remember the story in Exodus saved the Israelites from starvation as they wandered in the wilderness. Bread is a staple: time and time again in the Old Testament God uses bread to save the people.

This bread is the bread from heaven, bread which brings life now and forever. And all they have to do is eat it; all they have to do is believe.

It's both like and unlike our friends who ask what we would say at the gate of heaven.

Heaven, yes, whatever or wherever that might be, but certainly eternal life, but you don't have to get the right answer. Getting eternal life isn't about passing an exam, or even proving your worthiness. It's about being offered a plate of bread, taking a piece, and eating it. Even a child knows how to do that. And God will turn no one away who knows how to eat.

Which means us—and the whole world. For this bread Jesus gave for the life of the world, the bread of his flesh.

Here and now, in this world as in the next, God reaches out with bread to feed our souls, to bring us wholeness, to heal the world—so that we in turn may reach out, to bring to the world that same feeding and wholeness and healing.

And so we, here each Sunday, hang on for dear life to these peculiar rituals, reaching out empty hands for a piece of bread and the very life of God.

"Take, eat. This is my body broken for you. Do this in remembrance of me."

August 13, 2000—Proper 14, Year B
Deuteronomy 8:1–10; John 6:35–51
Trinity Episcopal Church, Princeton, New Jersey

There Is No doubt
A Sermon

Once upon a time there were three bears.

Once upon a time, there was a little girl and her name was Little Red Riding Hood.

Once upon a time there were three little pigs.

So begin all fairy tales, and as we hear those magical words "Once upon a time," we know that we are about to be ushered into a magical world where none of the rules apply, where frogs can talk, and bears eat oatmeal, and everything ends happily ever after.

These stories of our childhood, the stories which shape our world and tie us to the parents who sat by our beds reading in the soft yellow glow of the lamp, and to their parents, and to their parents before them, these stories have a special way of beginning, and we all know what to expect.

And today we hear once again another story, another story which shapes us, which ties us to the people who first told us, and to the people before them, today our story begins:

In the beginning, God created . . .

Not "once upon a time," but "in the beginning," before all time began.

There in the darkness is God. The earth is formless and void. Nothing moves. Nothing shines. Nothing sings. And there is God.

Most of us rush on, rush on to the day and the night; the earth and the sky; the sun, moon, and stars; and the earth as we know it. We rush on to plants and animals, and the human race, and speculations and arguments about creation and evolution, and how it is that our science and our religion can be made to fit.

But all the while there is God. Alone in the darkness.

And then God stirs.

"A wind from God swept over the face of the waters. And God spoke."

A wind from God, spirit, breath. A voice from God, and all things come to be. A new world, full of light and movement and song, like a bright spring morning after rain.

God exhales, and speaks breath and life into all creation. Breath and life into all creation, and breath and speech into you and me. There is no doubt. God is here.

The disciples are together again, Matthew tells us, one dead, dead by his own hand, eleven left, but none quite sure if the rumors and the visions had enough truth in them to outweigh the evidence of their own eyes, the stench of death, the cry of abandonment, that last rasping breath.

It was dark, not this time the darkness of a starless sky but the darkness of death, a death that tore the earth open, a death that tore the very hearts of his friends.

Together again, in the darkness, the disciples see a figure and wonder, hear the whisper of a voice, and know that it is true. Jesus is here again, risen, alive. "Go, disciple, baptize, teach. I am with you." His words give them new words: Make friends and introduce them to your friend who died and is alive, pour water on them, so that they know what it is to be cleansed and healed and forgiven, tell them about the God who loves them beyond their deepest dreams.

And when John tells the same story, the words come with a breath, a breath from God.

God in Christ exhales and speaks the breath of new life and new speech into his followers, into you, and me.

There is no doubt. God is here.

It is not so much later that the disciples are together again. This time there are more of them and the darkness is not so intense, though the waiting still confuses them, the fear still consumes them, they still don't know what it means to follow a dead, and risen but still gone, Savior.

They stand and wait and pray and wonder.

And then comes from nowhere a breath of wind, at first so gentle that it seems hardly real, then stronger and wilder until there can be no doubt that the breath of God has come again, come like that first wind of creation, and this time the speech comes from their very mouths— the words of God in every language for every person.

And around them the Parthians and the Medes, the Elamites and the Cappadocians, Italian, Greek, and Egyptian, men and women, black and white, young and old, all hear the voice of God as they have never heard it before.

God exhales, and speaks breath and words for all people. Breath and words, for you and me.

There is no doubt. God is here.

Years pass. Years upon years. The breath of God seems just a distant memory. The disciples, the followers of Christ gather again.

Another room, another city. They're a mixed bunch by now: They come from different places, believe different things. Some of them have been gathering there for years, others are brand new.

We are here. And the darkness gathers around us, just as it did around those other disciples so many years ago.

The darkness of a broken relationship.

The darkness of a body we can no longer depend upon.

The darkness of an uncertain future.

The darkness of a parish without a priest.

Sometimes it seems as if that darkness might overwhelm us.

But God is here.

God is here and the exhalation of God, the breath of life and speech, may be not so much like the blast of the whistle and the rattling rush of the Amtrak train hurtling down the middle tracks past my station, nor the fierce roaring wind of the tornado, sucking up lumber like dry autumn leaves.

But more like the feather-soft touch of the breeze on a warm spring day, the fleeting cool as the person sitting beside you exhales, or the gentle, holy kiss of an old friend.

God exhales, and speaks breath and words. Breath and words, into you and me, for you and me.

In the beginning God. Two thousand years ago, God. Here, today, in Riverside, God.

There is no doubt. God is here.

May 30, 1999—Trinity Sunday, Year A
Genesis 1:1–2:4a; 2 Corinthians 13:(5–10) 11–14; Matthew 28:16–20
St. Stephen's Memorial Episcopal Church, Riverside, New Jersey

NOTES

1. *Sermons by Hugh Latimer, Sometime Bishop of Worcester, Martyr, 1555,* ed. George Elwes Corrie (Parker Society Publications; Cambridge: University Press, 1844), 123. Latimer bases his argument on Romans 10:13–17.

2. Alexander Schmemann writes, "In separation from the word the sacrament is in danger of being perceived as magic, and without the sacrament the word is in danger of being 'reduced' to doctrine." In *The Eucharist: Sacrament of the Kingdom* (Crestwood, NY: St Vladimir's, 1987), 68.

3. "What's for Dinner?" *Circuit Rider,* September/October 2001, 32.

4. Latimer, *Sermons I,* 62.

5. *The Book of Common Prayer* (New York: Church Hymnal Corporation, 1979), 857–58.

6. "Of the Sacraments," Article 25 of the 39 Articles, *BCP 1979,* 872. These were derived during the Elizabethan period from the Edwardine 42 Articles.

7. John Macquarrie, *Principles of Christian Theology,* 2nd ed. (New York: Charles Scribner's Sons, 1977), 469.

8. Rowan Williams, *On Christian Theology,* Challenges in Contemporary Theology (Oxford, UK: Blackwell Publishers, 2000), 197.

9. David Brown and Ann Loades, "Introduction: The Divine Poet," in *Christ the Sacramental Word,* ed. David Brown and Ann Loades (London: SPCK, 1996), 19–20.

10. Charles Wesley, *Hymns on the Lord's Supper* (1745).

11. Paul Victor Marshall, *Preaching for the Church Today: The Skills, Prayer, and Art of Sermon Preparation* (New York: Church Hymnal Corporation, 1990), 78.

· 3 ·

Finding Our Way Home: Scripture

*E*very evening before I go to bed, I pick up a novel and read for half an hour or so. Most often it is a mystery—and as I read, I become immersed in that alternative world. Sometimes it has a historical setting, and I find myself compelled to find maps, history texts, biographies that will allow me to enter more fully into that time and place. Other more contemporary novels tend to use imaginary locations, so as not to interfere with real lives in real places. Either way, the world of the novel becomes real, and I frequently find myself wondering what is happening in that parallel book world as I go about my daily life. Even as I write, I'm anxious to get back to the world of P. D. James's newest offering, set on an imaginary island—or at least, it's not in my British road atlas—off the coast of Cornwall.

There are other sorts of reading. Each morning I open my computer and check the headlines from the *New York Times*, following up the two or three articles that provoke my interest. Lying in my front hallway is the instruction booklet for the new vacuum cleaner that I bought at the Thanksgiving sales. And in the living room is the biography of a friend from Australia, whom I know only as a gracious correspondent and elderly and gentle man of faith, but who, it emerges, was one of the "bright young things" of his day.

Whenever we open a Bible, we bring with us all these other experiences of reading. Different sections awaken memories of different experiences of reading—poetry, history texts, the stories we were read as children, the lists of rules posted on a swimming pool fence.

Often when I open my Bible to prepare to preach, I treat it like a newspaper or an instruction manual. I look for important facts, the essential information. Sometimes I'm tempted to treat it as biography, to learn more about its subject—a deeper level of knowing—or maybe even history. But what that does, in terms of my preaching, is reduce Scripture to a conveyor belt, passing a piece of information from one machine to another. Preaching can do better than that.

My strongest memories of reading the Bible as a child were of reading it as a story, alongside all the other stories that filled my bookcase and my library bag and my imagination. The imaginary world that those stories conjured up was as real to me as the one I lived in every day. Sometimes I wonder if, when I preach, I would be better to come to Scripture that way. When I read a novel, I do not consciously think, "this is fiction; it is imaginary." Rather, I approach it as a parallel world. The people assume three dimensions; I look up the details of their stories on maps and in history books. I live the text, as far as possible, "from the inside."

Of course, this approach has its limitations. The stories I read growing up and the novels I read today are intentionally fictional. The worlds they invite me into, the characters I meet, are intentionally artificial—albeit with enough connections to reality to make them believable. Approaching the scriptural text in preparation for preaching as if it were fiction undermines a primary claim of Scripture: This is reality! That does not mean it is simple history, something that can be proven true or false, empirically testable; rather, it bears witness to reality. It tells the story of human interaction with the divine through the eyes of people whose lives were changed by an encounter with the living God. There is no pretense of objectivity: the writers are deeply and personally involved with their stories. They are witnesses to truth, truth that may not be empirically verifiable, but truth all the same. It is this truth that we point to in our sermons, engaging with the world of Scripture in order to encounter God.

With this in mind I would like to suggest that when we open the Bible, when we turn to Scripture in preparation for preaching, we need a new kind of reading. It is one that enables us to find our home in this world of God's, reading that is both receptive and relational.

RECEPTIVE READING: ENTERING GOD'S WORLD

In a recent exhibition at the Fitzwilliam Museum in Cambridge, an illuminated manuscript of the Psalms was displayed. The Macclesfield Psalter is 250 leaves of beautiful illumination—precious stones ground fine to create vibrant pigments of blue and green and red and purple overlaid on hundreds, thousands even, of tiny marginal drawings that accompany the eloquent curves of gold and black lettering. Across the bottom of the page a farmer's wife chases a fox with a goose caught firm in his mouth and wrapped around his neck, a rabbit plays an organ in one corner while a monkey pumps the bellows, a dog-headed dragon breathes fire on a cowering lion. The attention paid to making this a work of art illustrates the importance Scripture held for the monastic community; the details of the illustrations, both realistic and fanciful, speak of an integral continuity between the world of Scripture and the world of everyday life.

When we open our Bibles, whether a beautifully bound and illustrated version like the Macclesfield Psalter or a more prosaic paperback with grainy black print, we enter a new world. It is a world where angels appear, healings occur, and visions are almost commonplace, a world where the main focus of life is the relationship between God and humanity and where God's intervention is rarely unexpected. Historically and geographically it is continuous with the world we live in; yet because Scripture continues to speak to us, to act as subject and not simply object, it also exists as a world in parallel with our own, a reality beyond the historical and geographical that we discover to be populated with our own heart's desires and fears. This is reality, as much as is our world of computers and friendships and quarrels and cars.

When Lucy steps through the wardrobe door into the magical world of Narnia, what she discovers is not an imaginary world, but a world as real as her own—and a world that becomes more real the more time she spends there. This discovery of a world more real intensifies until, in the final book in the *Chronicles of Narnia*, Lucy and all the characters we have come to know and love pass through a door and through a waterfall and come to a place that is the reality of which their own world was only a dim reflection.

So it is when we enter the world of Scripture. Inhabiting its world is not a retreat from reality, but an entering into deeper reality. And from this deeper reality, we gain a new perspective on the ordinary reality in which we live day by day.

The easiest way to approach this world of Scripture is as a tourist. When we arrive in a new country as a tourist, we usually want to visit the famous sights: the major monuments, great museums, natural wonders. We take photographs of key places, we learn enough of the language to deal with our basic needs, but mostly we rely on guidebooks and interpreters. We steer clear of discomfort, and, on returning home, relive our memories through photographs and reminiscences; we temporarily gain new perspectives, but they are soon overcome by ordinary everyday living.

When we approach Scripture as a tourist, we do exactly the same thing. We work our way down the list of must-see sites, the popular and the well-known. We take snapshots of our favorite Bible verses, and quickly move on from anything that makes us uncomfortable. We learn just enough of the language to deal with the basics—Christ, prophet, miracle—and leave the rest to the experts to worry about. And we return home, excitedly talking about what we have seen, but the excitement soon wears off and we go back to life as it had always been.

The second approach to Scripture, beloved of academicians, is that of the scientist. When we approach a country or culture with the primary intention of studying it objectively, we focus not on the tourist attractions, but on the minutiae of daily life. We observe, catalog, define, dissect, and analyze, frequently relying on the input of our professional peers. We are curious, fascinated by uniqueness, looking for patterns and connections to our own cultures. We plan to write papers and books, to share the knowledge we have uncovered, and to return home as "experts."

When we approach Scripture like a scientist, we focus on knowledge, putting the details together as a coherent whole. We explore the historical context, social structures, reliability of texts, issues of translation, and links with other texts. We turn to concordances, commentaries, and theologians for expert advice, and at the end of it all make a claim about what the text "means." The experience is, to a large extent, objective, and while faith may bring insight, it may just as easily be thought to cloud our interpretation. Our stance is that of a disinterested observer.

The third approach to Scripture—and the one that I believe is most useful for preachers—is that of the immigrant. When we come to a new country as an immigrant, we expect things to be different. We may have to learn a new language, or at least new vocabulary; there are different social expectations and cultural mores. To fit in, to belong, we have to adopt new clothing, accents, lifestyles. We never lose the culture of our homeland, but the longer we stay, the more aware we are of the differences. And as an immigrant, we invest in our new country; we develop relationships. We come to call it home.

When we approach Scripture as immigrants, we come expecting to inhabit this new world. We explore it as insiders, learning the culture and language not as observers but as practitioners. We are necessarily invested in it, with head and heart and soul. It is not enough to have technical skill or academic disciplines: Immigration demands our participation and commitment as people, practitioners, of faith. With such an approach, we cannot help but live what we preach. We live it from the inside. And in this living the text from the inside, in being immigrants and becoming residents, we find that Scripture itself challenges us. It demands certain beliefs, certain actions, certain faith of us. We cannot approach it this way and remain unchanged. And, if we are lucky, we fall in love—not just with our new home, but with the God who inhabits it.

But the most amazing thing is that as we become more at home in this new country, what we discover is that it is in fact our ancestral homeland, the place from which we originally came. Unknowingly we have been in exile; we came to this new place and made our home here, only to discover, paradoxically, that is has always been our home. And there is a second paradox. We are home, and yet we are not fully at home. This is the paradox of the kingdom of God—the now and the not-yet of it. This home has become a place of transformation, but it is one that always points us toward the final transformation, when we will finally be with God in the fullness of glory, God's and ours.

As a child, I naturally approached Scripture as a tourist: I went first for the stories—the classic snapshots of Moses in the bulrushes, Daniel in the lions' den, Jesus in the manger—supplemented as I grew older with the agony of Christ on the cross, doubting Thomas poking his hands in Jesus's side, and (my favorite) the gory details of Jael shoving a tent peg through Sisera's head. I learned to love these visits, and always took home a detailed report. When I went to seminary, I learned the tools of the scriptural scientist. Greek and Hebrew exegesis, historical criticism, sociocultural approaches to the text all served to fuel my understanding of the text. I learned to analyze, to understand, to interpret, to apply. My sermons stood on the firm foundation of competent exegesis. And that served me well for the first few years of my ministry.

But then things dried up. I read the text, and said "so what?" I checked out the commentaries, and tried to grab hold of a phrase that would serve as a theme for my sermon. I went back to old sermons from the previous cycles of the lectionary and reworked them for my current context. What resulted were sermons that were perfectly competent, but deprived of soul.

Then I went on sabbatical for six weeks and I paid attention to my soul, I prayed, I reflected, I lived in community, and I rediscovered the world of Scripture—and reading it became once again a joyous time of discovery. I began to return to my ancestral homeland, to see it with the eyes of the immigrant, and to make my home there.

It would be nice to think that we are all saturated in Scripture and prayer. But the reality is that, for many of us, that regular discipline is squeezed out by the routine demands and apparent emergencies that consume our lives. Often the only time we open our Bibles is when we have to write our weekly sermon. What I propose is an attentive, receptive approach to Scripture, in which we have a chance to open our souls to God.

We are invited into intimacy with God as we encounter God's active presence in the text. In writing on preaching the Old Testament, Ellen Davis quotes Flannery O'Connor on fiction, and it is equally applicable to our approach to Scripture: "Some people have the notion that you read the story and then climb out of it into the meaning, but for the fiction writer himself the whole story is the meaning, because it is an experience, not an abstraction."[1] When we climb into the text of Scripture and make ourselves a dwelling place there, the text—and God—becomes alive. We can encounter God.

Receptive reading is reading Scripture with this expectation. The text function as a kind of matchmaker, mediating the relationship between us and God, introducing us and reintroducing us in the hope that we will fall in love.

Love is wonderful. But as those who fall in love know all too well, sooner or later reality intervenes. This is a book about preaching, and our receptive reading does, perhaps unfortunately, have an end beyond falling in love. We have a sermon to write. And what that means, for most of us, is that we have to impose some sort of discipline on our reading.

So how do we do this receptive reading? One method is to use the insights of the tradition of *lectio divina*, that is, spiritual or divine reading.

Ad Verbum

Open my eyes, that I may perceive wondrous things in your law.
Take away, Lord, the veil from my heart, while I read the Scriptures.
Blessed are you, Lord; teach me your statutes.
Give me your Word, Word of the Father.
Touch my heart.
Enlighten the senses of my heart.
Open my lips, and fill them with your praise.
Be, O Lord, in my spirit and in my mouth.
In my mouth, that I might rightly and worthily proclaim your
pronouncements, by the holy-making power of your most Holy Spirit
O you, the coal of double nature, who touching the lips of the prophet, and
taking away his sin, touch my lips, I who am sin, and cleanse me from every
stain, and make me fit to proclaim your pronouncements.
O Lord, open my lips, and my mouth will proclaim your praise.
Lord, O Lord, give me learned language, that I might know what words I
should speak; and indeed any edifying word that is needed, that gives grace to
my hearers.
Grant that I might preach boldly.
Open my mouth, Lord: Fill me.

Lancelot Andrewes, 1555–1626[2]

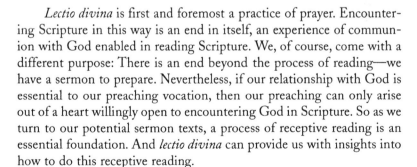

Lectio divina is first and foremost a practice of prayer. Encountering Scripture in this way is an end in itself, an experience of communion with God enabled in reading Scripture. We, of course, come with a
different purpose: There is an end beyond the process of reading—we
have a sermon to prepare. Nevertheless, if our relationship with God is
essential to our preaching vocation, then our preaching can only arise
out of a heart willingly open to encountering God in Scripture. So as we
turn to our potential sermon texts, a process of receptive reading is an
essential foundation. And *lectio divina* can provide us with insights into
how to do this receptive reading.

Lectio divina is an encounter, a conversation between us, Scripture,
and God. It is based on the assumption that, in Scripture, we can reliably meet God. Mario Masini, in his small book, *Lectio Divina: Ancient*

Prayer that Is Ever New, understands this reliability to be based on the incarnation. "The incarnation constitutes the historical-theological foundation for which 'the Word became flesh' is also 'the Word become book.'"[3] Incarnation is echoed in "inverbation": Christ is present in Scripture as in the Eucharist.

When we come to Scripture for the practice of *lectio divina*, we come with open minds. *Lectio divina* traditionally involved a fourfold process of reading and reflecting on the text: *lectio, meditatio, oratio,* and *contemplatio. Lectio* is reading. But it is a particular kind of reading: neither the reading we do for information nor that for recreation. Rather, it is reading for reception, a kind of attentive listening perhaps most like sitting on a sunporch listening to your grandmother's stories. You listen to find out your history, but you also listen because you are in relationship with one another, you listen to know your grandmother better, you listen because she loves you and that love pervades every word and because you love her. *Lectio* is reading, in the presence of the text and, inherently, in the presence of God.

The next step, *meditatio*, is resting in the presence of the text and of God. To continue the grandmother analogy, it's sitting beside each other on that sunporch in big comfortable armchairs, in silence, enjoying each other's company. We center on the text, allowing it to soak deep into our souls, its richness to drench us. It can be playful, this time of meditation, as we imagine ourselves into the story.

Oratio is when we begin to give voice to what is happening in our souls. It is the place of spontaneous, tentative, wondering utterance, words that issue from our hearts. Sitting on the porch, it is the language you stutter, "I love you, Grandma." "I love you, God."

And *contemplatio*, when you look at your grandmother there beside you on the porch and see the wrinkles wrought by the sun and lines by laughter and tears, and you see traces of your own features on hers, and you realize that you belong. We look at God and see the One in whose image we are made, and in whose image we are ever called to live.

When we do this sort of reflective, receptive soaking in the text, when we open ourselves through it to intimacy with God, we root our preaching in honest experience of God, with the unmistakable authenticity that brings.

But when we preach, our reading of Scripture cannot be shaped only by our own relationship with God. It is always something we do in relationship with the wider community. George Lindbeck's cultural-linguistic approach to doctrine provides us with a framework that both encompasses this intense, integral, personal relationship with the text and impels us to consider the text in wider relationship. He argues that religion is "a kind of cultural and/or linguistic framework or medium that shapes the entirety of life and thought"—much like the scriptural country in which I am an immigrant.[4] It is not, fundamentally, a system of beliefs or a symbolism of expression, but rather an organizing principle that encompasses these, an interpretive system that structures and shapes human experience and our understanding of our self and our world. What it looks most like, to Lindbeck, is a language—one with its own vocabulary of symbols and grammar that guides its use. "To become a Christian," Lindbeck writes, "involves learning the story of Israel and of Jesus well enough to interpret and experience oneself and one's world in its terms."[5] In other words, Scripture provides us with a framework for faith experience; it provides an external structure that we share with others, which enables us to interpret our internal experience of God.

Receptive reading is one part of our experiencing the text. But there is a second part: reading in relationship.

RELATIONAL READING: GOD IN OUR WORLD

One of the temptations for clergy is to read in isolation. We go into our studies, shut the door, and commune with God and the text. Meanwhile there is a whole world outside, ignorant of our self-appointed holy task. And that whole world extends not only across space but also across time. If our preaching is to engage our congregations, if it is to be a place where the connection between God and everyday life is made real, then we must read Scripture with a cognizance, an awareness, of that wider world of community and tradition.

One of the great discoveries of my seminary biblical education was the approach of canonical criticism. Finally I discovered a way to understand the essentially communal orientation of our texts and of our reading of them.

Canonical criticism addresses the question, "What is Scripture?" And its answer is that Scripture is a collection of writings that owe their authority to a process of reception and acknowledgment by a faith community itself informed and inspired by the Holy Spirit. The faith community—the early church—read these writings, and many others, and found that these texts in particular, over a period of time, were reliable in leading to an encounter with God, a deepening of faith. They were recognized as faithful witnesses to the "history of divine, redemptive intervention," to our encounter with God.[6]

Note what is missing here. There is no concern with empirical validation of the sources and intentions of the text, what the text *was*. Rather, the focus is on what the text *does*: It forms faith. Or, in the words of Brevard Childs, "The modern theological function of canon lies in its affirmation that the authoritative norm lies in the literature itself as it has been treasured, transmitted and transformed—of course in constant relation to its object to which it bears witnesses— and not in 'objectively' reconstructed stages of the process."[7] Scripture continues to bear witness for us: It is authoritative because it witnesses to reality. Our preaching is called to mirror this act of witness.

It is here that we begin to see the limits of my previous metaphor of immigration. In that metaphor, Scripture describes a world that is essentially complete in itself, into which we are invited to enter. But God cannot ever be confined in that way. Scripture cannot contain God, nor can it fully contain the things of God. Scripture is not self-referential: It always speaks of something beyond itself, always invites us to look beyond it to our God.

Therein lies a danger for us as interpreters. If Scripture is not complete in itself, then not everything for which we seek answers will be addressed in Scripture. Hence it can be dangerous to come to Scripture seeking specific answers; rather, we come open to the questions it directs back into the heart of our lives.

But there is a second implication of Scripture's otherwardness. While through it, we are invited to enter God's world, it is fundamentally the chronicle of God's entry into our world. It is not just we who shuttle between two worlds, it is God. God comes to us, just as God has always come.

It is relatively easy to see God at work in the world of Scripture, the world of God—whether we believe it or not. Within that self-referential framework, this God heals twisted limbs and turns water into wine and speaks from burning shrubbery. But as soon as we acknowledge that Scripture refers to something beyond itself, as soon as we admit to the possibility of a God whose actions can transcend the boundaries of geography and history, then we have admitted to a modicum of faith. Faith allows us to read Scripture and to recognize its paradigmatic quality for our own encounter with God today.

Often, when we set to work on our scriptural text, we begin by turning to technical tools. We read in one translation and then another; perhaps we open the Greek or Hebrew text and with the help of lexicons and commentaries try to work out what the words of the original text said and meant. This is important work. But for many of us, it is tempting simply to stop there.

Back in my undergraduate studies, I took a series of classes in statistical methods. I loved tinkering with numbers and watching patterns emerge from a muddle of undisciplined raw data. When it came to my final thesis on gender roles, self-esteem, and religiosity, I used statistical tests that even my professors had never heard of. But at the end of the year, my thesis came back with a comment something like this: "An interesting piece of research, but the meaning got lost in the analysis."

It's not that the traditional tools of historical, source, and redaction criticism—that focus on the words themselves in the way they became part of this thing we call Scripture—are unimportant; it's just that such study is merely the underpinning, not the whole of the interpretive process. Because Scripture always speaks of something beyond itself, we cannot make sense of it in isolation or abstraction: We constantly look for connections that will illuminate its meaning for us. There are multiple layers to this connection-seeking, relational reading. This first is reading scriptural texts in relation to the rest of Scripture.

Once again, a canonical approach provides useful insights into relational reading of Scripture. Childs argues that "attention should be paid to the canonical shape of the Gospels, that is to say, to the theological construal of the material which is reflected both in the process toward and in the final form of its literary composition."[8] The reason we pay attention to this canonical form, as preachers, is that our intention is first and foremost to proclaim the gospel, to invite encounter with the living God in the midst of everyday life; attending to the text in the form that we have received it helps us to avoid the trap of teaching details "behind" the text and inviting a technical rather than a relational approach to Scripture as the word of God.

So meaning is relational, multilayered, and complex. It resides not only in the words themselves, but in the interaction between those words, the form or genre in which they are contained, and the words that surround them—the chapter, book, testament, and whole of the Bible. When we read one of Jesus's parables, for example, we understand it in the context in which it is placed in Jesus's life, in its literary genre as parable, in its relation to other parabolic literature, in its placement in and relation to the Gospel in which it is recorded, in the New Testament, and in the whole of scriptural witness. What we find is a whole series of both overlapping and concentric circles, where the layers sometimes merge and sometimes bump against each other. In that process, they open to us a rich and complex web of meaning.

A second insight of the canonical approach is the emphasis on a communal model for interpretation, grounded in the church's role in the discernment or identification of the scriptural canon. Just as the early church used the way in which sacred writings enabled an encounter with God as a criterion for canonicity, so we as the church can expect to encounter God through canonical Scripture. Scripture is a reliable witness to the truth about God; preaching midwives encounter with the God of whom Scripture speaks. Once again that pushes us beyond a focus on Scripture itself per se, to the One of whom it speaks, that is, God.

The Church, emboldened by the Holy Spirit, discerned the canon of Scripture. We as preachers speak of that canon within the context of that churchly community. We are not unique or lonely bearers of testimony, but speak to and for our community, emboldened by that same Holy Spirit. And so, when we prepare to preach, we read Scripture in relationship with the church.

There are two aspects of this church-focused relational reading: reading in relationship with *the* church and reading in relationship with *our* church. Let me explain the difference between these.

Reading in relationship with *the* church is a reading that takes account of how this thing we call Scripture has been read in the full extent of the church, that extent being defined both historically and geographically.

The historical church is what we often call tradition—the context of generations upon generations of Christians reading this text. We come to it fresh, but we also come to it as one in a long line of readers and interpreters. It is important that we recognize the richness of that tradition, that interpretive lineage. We are not in this alone.

We can avail ourselves of these riches by reading the many primary sources that deal with our text. They range from the early church fathers and medieval theologians, many of whom left copious numbers of sermons and exegetical materials, through the Reformation commentators, who thanks to the invention of the printing press seem to have had printed almost every word they wrote or spoke, to more recent commentaries and preachers. For example, for the rare occasion when the Song of Songs sneaks into the lectionary,[9] why not reflect on Bernard of Clairvaux's mystical renderings or compare the sermons of the Anglican puritan George Gifford and the Anglican divine John Donne? We may not agree with the minutiae of their analysis—they speak from and to a different time and culture—but insofar as they read the same Scriptures that we read, which refer to one and the same God, we can glean riches from them. Obviously we can't do a major research project on every text that we preach—even the most committed preachers among us cannot devote our whole lives to sermon preparation—but we can make a practice of dipping into these historical resources, and allowing them to remind us of the many ways of reading Scripture.

Having read in relationship with the church historical, we turn to the church today. With the caveat I mentioned earlier, about staying aware of our churchly context and not getting buried in the details, we now turn to commentaries, where we can read a thoughtful academic reflection on the text and gain insight into the linguistic, historical, cultural, and theological forces that have shaped both the text and its interpretation. Commentaries, of course, vary in scope and emphasis. Some require a knowledge of Greek or Hebrew, and/or focus largely on linguistic issues. Others focus more on theological themes or the historical and cultural contexts; some take a thematic rather than verse-by-verse approach; still others are oriented toward preaching, whether structured around a particular book or to follow the lectionary. All are useful resources for the preacher.

What is key about this kind of reading is that we are seeking not simply to uncover the text as object, but to find out how others have engaged it and to let the richness of that engagement inform our preaching.

Reading in relationship with the wider church also means exploring the ways in which the church in other traditions and other places reads the text. Visit a theological library and you will find shelf after shelf of sermons, missionary biographies, and commentaries that give insight into the ways others have interpreted Scripture across time and place. There is an enormous richness to be found there.

However, most of us are no longer totally dependent on access to a library: The Internet has placed vast resources at our disposal. We merely have to go online to see how someone in Adelaide, Australia, has preached on our text; we can find both liberal and conservative perspectives on blogs; we can draw on the expertise of scholars in online journals. Many sites offer exegetical tools, reflections on texts, or sermons—some contemporary, some historical. Of course, not all sites are equal. Anyone can publish a website; you need no credentials. Just because someone offers exegetical reflections does not mean that their work has a sound academic foundation; there are as many bad sermons online as good ones. Two ways of searching out the good from the bad are the following:

- Use a search engine to find out about the website owner. What church do they belong to? Do they have anything published in dead-tree form, and, if so, by whom? Who else links to them?
- Examine what other resources they reference (in footnotes or links in the text, or in a links section of the website).

The Internet also allows us to share with our peers our own encounter with the text: I belong to a preaching e-mail list based in England, where we share our ideas, struggles, and discoveries. Some clergy have blogs and invite parishioners to contribute and respond to their reflections. These can be immeasurably enriching processes.

The Internet allows us to easily access the perspectives of others from across the world. However, there is a danger here. It is so easy to find voices we like online that we limit our wider reading, that we read only people who think like we do. We are not really hearing the wider church, just our own opinions repeated ad infinitum. Our richest insights are likely to come when we listen to voices unlike our own, when our theology is honed by the challenge and question of the other.

And so I try on a regular basis to read something by someone with whom I might ordinarily expect to disagree, whose perspective is markedly different from my own. I trust that if they love God, if they are open to the Holy Spirit, then perhaps they will have insights that I may miss—or, at least, they will give me something to argue against!

Reading in relationship with the church also invites us to consider how our Scriptures are being read in our own communities and in communities other than our own. We frequently turn to commentaries for this purpose, not just to gain an expert perspective, but to see a broader, more objective view of what the text is saying. The simplest part of this, it would appear, is to find out how this Scripture is read in our own community—and yet this is a step that is frequently omitted in our sermon preparation. A few weeks ago, I was driving two children from my congregation to our diocesan acolyte festival. Given that I had a sermon to write, I asked them to read the passage aloud as I drove, and then we talked about it. And what emerged was a wonderful discussion of how it is that God can heal. With their permission, that conversation became the foundation for the next morning's sermon. Likewise, I still remember a conversation with a teenage member of the parish I served in ten years ago. We were sitting outside in the sun—the rest of her Sunday School class hadn't shown up—talking about Luke 14:34: "Salt is good; but if salt has lost its taste, how can its saltiness be restored?" She said, "But if salt isn't salty, then it isn't salt." It seems obvious. But those of us who have grown up in the church and heard that passage read and preached numerous times easily forget the obvious. Once again, a conversation became the basis of my sermon.

There are many ways we can garner the perspectives of our own faith community. The most structured is to have a group that meets regularly—weekly or monthly—with the specific purpose of discussing the texts for upcoming Sundays. Such groups typically include those who will preach, along with a representative selection of congregation members, people who are thoughtful about their faith and who represent the diversity of the congregation—in terms of age, gender, race, political perspective, and so forth. Such groups can be a rich resource for our preaching.

But sometimes such groups are not possible, whether because of time constraints, the traditions of the church, or a simple reluctance of people to participate. Another way to gain at least some community perspective is to imagine how different members of the congregation would hear the text—an elderly pillar of the church, a newcomer hesitantly trying church after years of estrangement, a father who doesn't quite know what he believes but comes for the sake of the family, a child as alight with joy at the rich vestments and shiny communion vessels and knowing she is loved, or a teenager trying to work out whether this faith is truly their own anyway. Imagine what details would catch their attention. What would perplex them, what would excite them?

Of course, to do this, you need to know your congregation. We preachers get to stand up front and talk to people all the time; they know what we think, and they often see us at our most passionate, our most fulfilled. To know our people, we need to give them the same opportunities to share their lives, their faith, their passions and joys and struggles. I try to visit regular parishioners—not just those in crisis—whenever I can, to see them in the places where their hearts are. We share meals, coffee, gym time, even shopping! Then I can begin to have a sense of who they are, how God might speak to them through the texts.

And finally, take every opportunity to talk with members of your congregation about the Scriptures and about what you plan for the sermon. Car trips, work days, conversations over coffee, all are prime opportunities to ask for their opinions—and they will usually be flattered to be invited to participate in the preaching process. Observe how these texts shape their lives. You cannot use their example directly in the sermon without asking specific permission, but often their lives will open up ideas for parallels that have the ring of truth.

But relational reading of Scripture is not confined to reading in relationship with the church; we also read in relation to the ordinary world that we live in. Whenever we read a text, we will be assailed by associations—events that have occurred, things we have read or seen on TV, people we know, all the myriad of things that influence our lives and thought. Our culture and experience are always present and influence us, and much as we might like to be left to read in peace, to be able to develop some abstract understanding of what the text *really* means, that is impossible. We do not live in a vacuum: We always read in the context of real life.

And so, when I read the story of John the Baptist, I read it with all the baptisms I have ever celebrated forming pictures in my mind. I recall the joyous "yes!" of a four-year-old in answer to the question, "Do you want to be baptized?" and the gentle slosh of the water being poured into the font, the soft weight of a baby's head in my hand. When

I read the Old Testament lesson for Trinity Sunday, I am transported to a Presbyterian church in Melbourne, Australia, with its sloped seating and high pulpit, where I preached on behalf of the young-adult group one of my first sermons, entitled "The Uncomfortable Pew," and I wonder once again what God is calling me to. When I hear Psalm 40, my mind echoes with the refrain of U2's "40": "How long?"

We can't help but read with these associations echoing in our minds. Sometimes we put them aside to use later as "illustrations," but the reality is that they continue to lurk in the background, shaping the way we think about the text. Of course, it works both ways, such as when we refer to our legal code and find buried in it echoes of the Levitical laws, when we read a poem and recognize allusions to Scripture.

Life influences our reading of Scripture; our reading of Scripture influences life. Philosophers call this interrelatedness "intertextuality." Everything we say is drawn from and comprised of other things that have been said. When we read, what we read is shaped by the things the writer had read and heard, and what we understand is shaped by what we have read and heard before. None of it is entirely new; it's like one of those kaleidoscopes where by turning the end you create a new pattern, but every pattern is implicit in what has gone before. Meaning is the result of the collision and influence of everything we have ever heard, read, or experienced. Some of these collisions and influences are subtle, barely noticeable; others cannot be ignored and demand our attention.

So when we read Scripture, we read it alongside all the other "texts" that twist and turn in our minds. They come from our education, our relationships, our family history, the media, our interactions with the world around us, crashing into and bumping against and embracing the text, so that what we have is not just ink on a page, but a living, breathing thing in which, somehow, we recognize the voice of God.

In practice, it helps to be aware of this intertextual dimension. When some memory impinges on our reading, we can stop and ask: Why am I thinking about this? What is it saying about the text? How might the text speak to it? Where is God here? And often those questions are the key to what we end up preaching.

～◯

Encountering the Text
Preliminaries

- Find a quiet, holy space—a room, outside, an empty church. Anywhere that breathes freedom and holiness.
- Invite God to be present: "Blessed Lord, who hast caused all holy Scriptures to be written for our learning; Grant that we may in such wise hear them read, mark, learn, and inwardly digest them, that by patience, and comfort of thy holy Word, we may embrace, and ever hold fast the blessed hope of everlasting life" (*Book of Common Prayer* [1662], Collect for the Second Sunday in Advent).

Receptive Reading

- Read the text for the first time. Read it aloud. Let the language play on your lips, the words float across your consciousness. Don't worry too much about understanding—just read with an open heart and soul.
- Imagine yourself in the text. Who are you? How do you feel? With whom do you identify?
- Allow your own questions to surface. What are you confused about? What are you uncomfortable with? What would you like to ask God?

Relational Reading

- Engage in conversations with Scripture: Explore the context of the text.
- Have conversations with the church: Explore historical resources, commentaries, exegetical tools, sermons, and others' reflections on the text.
- Hold conversations with your church: Talk about the text with members of your community, imagining how they would read it.
- Participate in conversations with the world: What connections can you see between the text and your life, the news (both local and global), other media, pop culture, or social and cultural trends?

Gather all your explorations together and let them rest in your mind, allowing a time of waiting before beginning the actual work of preparing the sermon itself.

～◯

HOLDING IT ALL TOGETHER

Receptive reading and relational reading are two ways of engaging with Scripture, two ways of engaging with God. Paradoxically, when we do these two kinds of reading, we both enter into God's world, as if to a new country, and find God's presence and activity in our own world. The dream, of course, is that the two are one and the same—God's world is our world. But that is a vision of the new creation, a vision of glory. Meanwhile, we live in a context where there is a disjunction, a crevasse, between the two. Theologically speaking, that's the fall—a rupture between the world of God and the world of human experience that we have been ever since trying to heal. The death of Christ bought about the healing of that rupture, but we only taste it now; we will experience it in full in glory.

Enough conversation. Sooner or later we have to return to the text, to read it, sit with it, reflect on it, and, guided by the Holy Spirit, begin to make sense of it in relation to our congregation and our world.

Grace Comes
A Sermon

It's one of those stories where we're never quite sure whose side we're supposed to be on.

On the one hand there's Naaman. A rich man, a powerful man, a man of substance, but tormented by a terrible disease. It began with just a patch of skin that went a strange color: pale, kind of like a burn blister, but he hadn't been burned. And then he noticed that when he poked at it, he couldn't feel anything. And it began to spread. He didn't realize he'd injured his hand until he noticed it was infected, and by then the bone and the cartilage and skin had scarred and stiffened and twisted. And he began to limp, and his vision blurred as the grit and sand and sun scarred his dried-out corneas.

He was a powerful man, and by insisting on his privacy and taking refuge in the excuse of busyness he had been able to hide it, but it was becoming impossible, and already his wife and servants had guessed and begun to keep their distance.

His body had become disfigured and his relationships as well, and the disease and disfigurement were spreading to his soul.

It was only by chance that out of all the captives that he'd taken in military action, out of all of them, he'd kept one slave to work in his household, a private attendant for his wife.

It was only by chance that that young girl had heard of a man back in her homeland, had heard of a man who could work miraculous things, make food from near nothing, purify things that had gone bad, even raised a child from death; this young girl, this slave had heard of the prophet who maybe could even heal leprosy.

And it was only by chance that instead of holding that knowledge close, sullen and resentful, carrying a secret that made her more powerful than her disfigured owner, instead of that, she wondered aloud in the hearing of her mistress, if maybe the prophet might be able to help.

It was only by chance, by chance—or perhaps by the grace of God.

Either way, Naaman took the chance. Being a rich man, a powerful man, a man of substance, he went first to the king. Diplomatic channels were the way to get things done: a letter of introduction, copious gifts, and of course all the weight of influence of the official representative of a powerful nation graciously visiting a weaker state. It was the obvious thing to do.

And so he arrived at the door of the king of Israel, laden with gold, silver, clothing, a letter of introduction, and a plea. The problem was that the king of Israel had no idea what Naaman was talking about. Healing? Miracles? The king couldn't do any of that. And he began to panic.

Naaman, meanwhile, was getting impatient. He was an army man. What was this petty king fussing about? Surely he knew what was going on in his country, under his command. Any good soldier would. On the other hand . . . maybe this was why his own army's repeated raids on Israel's lands had met with little resistance.

But then a message came from a prophet. And next thing, Naaman was out the door, with his horses and chariots and gold and silver and fine clothes, on his way to see this prophet of Israel.

But the prophet didn't even come out to meet him. He just sent a message for Naaman to go wash in the Jordan. And Naaman was not impressed. "I'm offering you a king's ransom, and you tell me this? Why should I with all my power, all my money, why should I go wash in that dirty stream you call a river?"

That's Naaman.

And then there was Elisha. He's supposed to be the hero, I guess. After all, he was the one chosen by God, passed the mantle, the authority, the power, the reputation of the great prophet Elijah. He did his miracles: an everlasting container of oil, stagnant water turned pure, a dead child brought back to life. He had all the God-credentials. But there was something about him that just wasn't very likable.

He had heard about this military man, come from a warring tribe with his letter of introduction, his gold and silver and fine clothing, he heard about him and sent to him. But when Naaman arrived, instead of going out to greet him as hospitality would demand, Elisha just sat inside his house. Not even a glass of water to cool the visitor's parched tongue. Instead he sent a messenger, a servant. "Go wash in the Jordan seven times."

Naaman was understandably offended. But one servant summoned up his courage and said to Naaman, "You know, it's worth a chance. What have you got to lose?" And eventually Naaman went and did what he was told, and stepped out of the water with his body as strong and beautiful as it had ever been.

It wasn't until Naaman got back to the prophet's hut that Elisha was willing to see him; even then the prophet was ungracious, refusing the gifts Naaman pressed upon him. And later, when the prophet's servant sneaked after Naaman and asked for just a tiny fraction of what Naaman had offered (after all, he deserved a reward—he'd been the one that had to go tell a mighty warrior to wash in a muddy stream), Elisha condemned him and cursed him with Naaman's leprosy.

Naaman. Elisha. They're two of a kind—autocratic, imperious men of great power. Naaman is convinced money can buy anything. Elisha is convinced that his prophetic power, his prophetic pedigree granted by the mantle of Elijah, gives him license to act as he pleases. We can find excuses for their behavior, but the reality is that there is nothing very likable in either of them. Neither is likely to become our hero. And I don't particularly want to be on the side of either one. In fact, to be honest I'd really rather lavish my attention on that young slave who first dared tell her mistress about the healing prophet or those courageous servants who dared tell the angry Naaman to go wash in the Jordan. They are worthy of honor.

Except that I suspect that it is Naaman and Elisha who are more like us. Like Naaman we are full of our own importance. We might like to think of ourselves as humble, but in reality we expect to be considered important enough to get full, direct, personal attention from God. And if we don't, we tend to either stand outside and rage, or turn and walk away. Never mind that God sends messengers, never mind that God is known to be trustworthy. We want what we want and we want it now.

And like Elijah we know the authority of our pedigree. Sometimes we forget to be gracious; sometimes we forget that it is really God at work in us and that we do nothing on our own. We are proud, and we let no one forget it.

But you know what? You know what? God is at work, even in spite of us. God is at work even when we are arrogant, full of our own self-importance. Neither Elisha nor Naaman did anything at all to make them worthy of God's attention, God's grace. But God blessed them anyway, and made them part of something far, far bigger than they could ever have imagined—so that Naaman is remembered this day not because of his power and wealth but because God healed him; Elisha is remembered not because of his pedigree but because he became the agent of God's healing. Grace comes, but it comes so often not because of but in spite of us, grace comes and it doesn't obey the rules, grace comes and it is a source of blessing.

Nothing we do deserves it. Nothing we do deserves it. We step forward and suddenly we are in a new world, and God is among us. Not chance, but the grace of God.

February 12, 2006—Epiphany 6, Year B
2 Kings 5:1–14
Trinity Episcopal "Old Swedes" Church, Swedesboro, New Jersey

Nativity to Resurrection
A Sermon

One of my favorite children's books is called *The Nativity*.[10] It's the story of Jesus's birth taken straight from the King James Version of the Bible, but illustrated by a woman called Julie Vivas, who paints watercolors that the people who translated the King James Version could never have imagined. On the very first page, we are introduced to the angel Gabriel. Instead of appearing in Renaissance glory, tall and handsome, with gold-leafed wings, pristine white robes, and a serene expression on his face, this Gabriel's wings are yellow and pink and blue and green and purple, with tears in the ends where he's damaged them in crash landings, and his brown hair sticks up every which way. His greenish-blue robe has holes in the knees, and on his feet are big clumpy hiking boots with the laces untied. He's the sort of angel who crashes into trees and sits at the kitchen table with a mug of coffee, who goes sheep riding when he's supposed to be concentrating on bringing good news to the shepherds and dangles from a branch in order to talk with camels at their eye level. And at the end of the story, there he is, holding the baby Jesus while his poor mother Mary tries to get back up on the donkey.

Now fast-forward thirty-three years. Because I have a sneaking suspicion that it's the same angel who appears at the tomb on Easter morning. We don't know for sure, but any angel who appears at the tomb, pushes back the stone, and then sits down on top of it has to have more in common with the angel that I remember from that book of the Nativity than with your typical Renaissance angel who looks like he wouldn't move a muscle for fear of getting his clothes dirty or his wings bent. The angel in Matthew's account of the resurrection seems to have swapped his blue-green robe for a white one, but already it has some mud on the hem and a bit of a rip where he put his shoulder to the stone to push it aside, and there's a damp patch at the back where he sat down on the dew-covered grass for a rest halfway through rolling the stone back. And he's a bit sweaty, and as usual, his hair is sticking up everywhere and his wings a little the worse for wear. And he still hasn't learned to tie his bootlaces. He pushes and he pushes, and it's no wonder that when he's done, he climbs up on that stone and sits down for a rest.

And if that's the angel who is at the tomb, early that first Easter morning, then I imagine the rest of the scene isn't quite the way most artists picture it.

The sun has just come up, and two women come, Mary Magdalene and another Mary, hunched over and wearing dingy old clothes, the sort that let you kind of blend into the shadows, and their eyes are red and bloodshot from crying, and even though they've washed their faces, you can still see the trails the tears have made. No beautiful garden, but a rough rock face with a hole, and mud where they had trampled getting his body in. And beside it two guards, resentful at being given such a stupid job, guarding a dead man, and playing cards to while away the time.

Suddenly the earth begins to tremble and shake, and the two women grab onto each other to stay upright, and with a flash of light, the angel crash-lands in front of the tomb and begins pushing the stone back. The guards are so shocked that they faint, so the angel has to work around them, and by the time he's done he's so exhausted that he climbs up onto the stone to take a rest. And then he notices the women, still frozen in shock, and says, "Sorry about that. Don't be afraid. If you're looking for Jesus, he's risen—take a look for yourselves. And then go, go quickly and tell the rest of his friends that it's all okay, that they should make for Galilee and they'll find him there."

So the two women turn and run, half in fear, half in joy, almost tripping over in their excitement. And then suddenly right in front of them is a man. His clothes are as multicolored as the angel's wings, all pink and yellow and green and blue and purple blending into one gorgeous rainbow of color, his skin fresh and new like a newborn baby's. But his voice, his voice they know. It's Jesus. And they fall on their faces and grab hold of his feet, and he tells them, "Get up, look at me! I'm no longer dead! I'm alive! I'll meet you all in Galilee. Tell everybody!"

The colors of his life wash over them, and suddenly they are no longer teary, red-eyed mourners in dingy clothing, but transformed, their clothing washed golden in the light of his life, their faces lit up with joy, reflecting a world that has suddenly burst into color, glowing with the message, "Christ is risen!"

That's the way I imagine it would look if Julie Vivas took it into her head to illustrate this story. It would look real. And that's what's so important about this picture-book version. Because most times, when we see pictures of how people imagine the resurrection, it's not really believable. Everyone looks perfectly composed, their clothing well ironed, their faces clean, the scenery as if it had been designed by an expert landscape gardener. There is no tragedy of death lurking in the background, no cross standing vigil against the sky.

But if the Gospels are anything to go by, the resurrection, if it was nothing else, was real. As real as the pain, as real as the suffering, as real as the despair that all of us know goes along with the death of someone we love. They had watched Jesus die, had seen the thorns drip blood down his face, the nails tear at his hands and feet, the spear rip into his side. They'd been there when he breathed his last, gasping breath, when the earth had shaken the first time, and the rocks shuddered into pieces. They'd been there when they took his body down, and wrapped it in a cloth, and put it in a stone-hewn tomb. This was real. There was no doubting it. Jesus was dead.

That's why the two on their way to Emmaus didn't recognize him at first. That's why Thomas couldn't believe it when the other disciples told him they'd seen Jesus. That's why the disciples didn't believe the women the first time they told them that Jesus was risen. His death was real.

And so was his resurrection. When Jesus came out of the tomb, it wasn't just a figment of their imaginations, a bit of wishful thinking from people who would have been better off staying home till they got over their grief. This wasn't a beautiful scene from a Hallmark card: This is real. Life at its fullest, life with the same intensity that you find in a new baby, the same energy as a young child. This is life, life so strong that it's infectious, raw, powerful, life-giving.

People were in shock, unable at first to believe the evidence of their own eyes. Stumbling around, uncertain, and then shock giving way to joy, as the wonder of it all dawned upon them, as they discovered their lives transformed by the irresistible life of the risen Lord.

And it's still real. Jesus is still risen. And still his life is powerful enough to transform our lives, his life is irresistible enough that we can't help but be drawn in. "Come," he says. "Follow me! Death has lost the battle, and life has won! Tell everybody! Alleluia!"

Sunday, March 27, 2005—Easter Day, Year A
Matthew 28:1–10
Trinity Episcopal "Old Swedes" Church, Swedesboro, New Jersey

NOTES

1. Flannery O'Connor, "The Nature and Aim of Fiction," in *Mystery and Manners*, by Flannery O'Connor, ed. Sally and Robert Fitzgerald (New York: Farrar, Straus and Giroux, 1969), 73, cited in Ellen F. Davis, *Wondrous Depth* (Louisville, KY: Westminster John Knox Presss, 2005), 9.

2. From Lancelot Andrewes, *Preces privatæ quotidianæ* (Oxford: J. H. Parker, 1853), 354–55, my translation.

3. Mario Masini, *Lectio Divina: Ancient Prayer that Is Ever New* (New York: Alba House, 1998), 6.

4. George Lindbeck, *The Nature of Doctrine* (Philadelphia: Westminster, 1984), 32.

5. Lindbeck, *Nature of Doctrine*, 34.

6. Brevard S. Childs, *Biblical Theology of the Old and New Testaments: Theological Reflection on the Christian Bible* (Minneapolis: Fortress Press, 1992), 73.

7. Childs, *Biblical Theology*, 71.

8. Childs, *Biblical Theology*, 605.

9. Song of Solomon 2:8–13 is scheduled to be read in the Revised Common Lectionary on Proper 9A/Ordinary 14A and Proper 17/Ordinary 22B.

10. Julie Vivas, *The Nativity* (Adelaide: Omnibus Books, 1986).

· 4 ·

Strangers at Home: Hospitality

$\mathcal{A}$ single arch remains, fragile against the sky, almost at odds with the stolid magnificence of the carved pillars that line one side of the nave. Almost a thousand years of touch have shaped this place, first hewing the stone, hefting it into place, then the brush of worshippers as they passed through doors and leaned against walls, followed by wind, salt, rain, and finally the sometimes wondering, sometimes complacent oil of tourist fingers working its way into the rock. A block of stone carved in Anglo-Saxon times to hold the shaft of a cross, then split in two and reused in the Norman priory, is now the resting place for a pigeon, fluffed out against the cold, either too tame or too ill to move when I gently stroke its feathers with my finger. It is a place of hospitality once more.

That is what is so striking about this place. A Benedictine foundation, built on the site of Celtic ruins here at the edge of the world, an island off the coast of an island, a place, it sometimes seems, forsaken by all except God—and the summer tourists. But when winter closes in, it reverts to its true self, a place of barren extremes. Cut off from the mainland two times a day, mud flats and quicksand, grassy dunes and rocky outcrops, it has nevertheless sustained a small community for at least fourteen hundred years—raising cattle and tanning hides for parchment, fishing, producing lime, raising sheep—and welcoming the thousands of pilgrims and tourists who come this way and have always come, following Aidan and Cuthbert and Cedd. Rooted in Celtic Christianity and sustained in the Benedictine way it welcomes without question those who come, pilgrim and tourist alike, and invites them to encounter the Holy One.

All guests who present themselves are to be welcomed as Christ, who said, "I was a stranger and you welcomed me" (Matt. 25:35). Proper honor must be shown "to all, especially to those who share our faith" (Gal 6:10) and to pilgrims . . . with all the courtesy of love. (*Rule of Benedict*, chapter 53)

Hospitality is a core Christian practice. Yet all too often it has been eclipsed by a private piety that focuses on withdrawal from the world. Much of Christianity in the modern period has been characterized by such an inward orientation. Even the growth of social justice ministries in the twentieth century often owes more to the donors' pietistic desire to give than to the recipients' real need. True hospitality, by contrast, demands a focus that is outward, a willingness not only to invite but to wholeheartedly welcome others into our space, placing their comfort above our own. Offering food and shelter—practical action—is the most obvious expression of hospitality. But it is also expressed in many other contexts, and is of central importance in preaching.

Hospitable preaching invites listeners in, welcoming them without reservation, without question. Unhospitable preaching keeps them at a distance. When a sermon excludes hearers, it has the net effect of saying: This church, this faith, is not for you. Hospitable preaching reaches out to stranger and nonstranger alike. It offers space, welcome, a place of safety in which we may encounter God.

MONASTIC AND SCRIPTURAL INSPIRATIONS

The Rule of St. Benedict is unequivocal in its demand that the monastic community exercise hospitality. Where monasticism in its earliest forms tended to be characterized by solitude and extreme asceticism, Benedict's rule was practical, communal, and oriented toward the world.

That had not been Benedict's original intention. He was born around 480, in Nursia, Italy, when the world was falling apart. Rome had been sacked, the empire was in ruins, and there was no longer any secular legal structure to guide and protect the people. Meanwhile, the church too was in ruins, torn apart by doctrinal dispute, moral compromise, and persecution. Disgusted with life in Rome, Benedict resolved to become a hermit, and took himself off to live in a (relatively) isolated cave. His pietistic plans were soon subverted—it's difficult to be a hermit when people keep gathering around to share your life! After twenty-five years or so, Benedict took his followers and founded an intentional community at Monte Cassino; it was in this experience of community that his rule emerged. As DeWaal notes, Benedict held together the solitary and the community, spirit and world.[1] And in a time when hospitality was necessary to a traveler's survival, he opened his community to all manner of people, from the greatest to the least, in the name of Christ. In this he was following his Christian forebears, who in the early centuries of the faith were renowned for the extraordinary quality of their hospitality—a foundational Christian value.

This extraordinary hospitality was hardly an innovation of the Christian church. It was one of the legacies of the Jewish tradition taken up by the early Christians, and given new life in the name of Christ. The urging of Hebrews, "Do not neglect to show to show hospitality to strangers, for doing that some have entertained angels without knowing it" (Hebrews 13:2), alludes to the story of Abraham, camped by the oaks of Mamre (Genesis 18:1–10). Abraham offers hospitality to three passing strangers; it is in their words of promise that it becomes clear that these are not men, but angels, messengers speaking on behalf of God.

The possibility of entertaining angels is a strong motivator to hospitable action; it becomes even more urgent with Christ's words as reported in Matthew 25:25: "I was a stranger and you welcomed me." This is not just the one-in-a-million chance that these strangers might be angels in disguise; this is the certainty that in every single person whom we welcome, we welcome Christ himself.

And if that were not sufficient motivation, there is a second strand in Scripture. In Deuteronomy 10:19, the people are commanded to welcome/befriend/love the stranger who lives among them because they know what it is to be strangers.[2] It sounds great—unless you happen to be a fairly small community that has just invaded the land, thrown out or killed its inhabitants, and set up your own principality. Strangers were dangerous. Strangers could be spies. At the very least, strangers brought with them their own traditions and religious practices, an alternative to the worship of YHWH. Strangers threatened not just the homogeneity but also the religious faithfulness of the people of Israel. And yet the Torah is adamant: The people are not just to welcome, but to love strangers, offering them acceptance and friendship in place of fear and rejection. Why? Because they know what it is to be strangers. And they know what it is to receive grace.

God loves strangers. Time after time God chooses the outsiders, the unimportant, the forgotten, and showers them with blessing. It was true for the Jewish people; it was true of Christ. The Gospel of Luke in particular shows Christ repeatedly reaching out to those who don't belong, in one way or another, those who are strangers in their own communities, those who are strangers to faith. They might be diseased or despised, women, tax collectors, sinners. But Jesus welcomes them, even when nobody else will.

Perhaps that's our problem. Most of us in the church have forgotten what it was like to be strangers—to each other and to God. The church is home for us: It has become a place of refuge, where we know one another and are known.

And that makes it all the more imperative for us to be aware of the strangers who come among us—those who tentatively step in the door, lured by some dimly remembered sense of peace from childhood or simple curiosity or even more basic need. For them, these are strange places, full of promise but also of threat. What if I do something wrong? What if my children misbehave? Or, perhaps unacknowledged, that childhood fear: What if they don't like me?

We all remember what it was like in childhood to be the last one picked for a team, the odd one out, the only one without the coveted birthday invitation. That's exactly what it's like for strangers coming to church. And God calls us not just to tolerate them, or even to make them comfortable—to show them the bathrooms and find the right page and give instructions about the Eucharist and settle the children— but to love them. It's a deeply personal, deeply intimate thing.

But sometimes that's the easy part. Strangers have no history with us; they have no claim on us. We welcome them without obligation. But the demands of hospitality extend to those whom we know. "Welcome one another, therefore, just as Christ has welcomed you, for the glory of God" (Romans 15:7). It could hardly be more clear: Hospitality must be exercised to those *within* the community of faith as well as to those outside it. And that is often much more difficult than welcoming strangers. When we know people, we know their foibles and faults as well as their strengths. We remember the petty—and grand—hurts, even as we remember the joys and celebrations. It takes a deliberate decision to be hospitable to those whom we know—our enemies, friends, and the many in between—as well as humility, the willingness to forgive, and a good dose of grace.

WELCOME HOME: GATHERING THE PEOPLE OF GOD

There is nothing quite like coming home. Whether it's from a day at work, a week's vacation, or a long absence of many years, when we turn the corner, when we open the door, there is a visceral reaction. Even when our homecoming is fraught with tension, we can know deep down that this is the place where we belong.

The place where we grew up, the places we now live—they are one kind of home. But there is another kind of home deeply embedded in our souls—the longing for home with God. It is this sense of home that Augustine evokes in his famous phrase, "Our hearts are restless, O God, until they find their rest in Thee." All of us long for God; we long for that sense of belonging. The power of the parable of the prodigal son is that it makes the connection for us between our experience of a familial home—and all the tensions with which that can be fraught—and our home in God, with its unquestioning, unconditional welcome.

Hospitable preaching is like the father, rushing with open arms toward the prodigal son. It says to the hearers, "Welcome home." It is not so much a matter of content—I'm not talking about evangelistic sermons here—so much as style, not what we communicate, but how. And there are two things of central importance in welcoming our hearers home: cultural context and language.

Cultural Context

There is no such thing as a generic sermon. The same words, preached at a different time or in a different place, have different power. They will connect in different ways; they will evoke different things; they will rise and soar or fall down flat at different points. All this points to the reality that preaching is an interactive art—the words on the page are not absolute; their meaning is derived, at least in part, from the context in which they are heard. And the context in which they are heard will determine whether they are heard as welcoming or distancing.

～○

Knowing Your Context

Nothing can replace knowing the cultural context of your congregation. We as preachers need to be deliberate about it. In her book, *Preaching as Local Theology and Folk Art,* Leonora Tubbs Tisdale provides a rich guide for exegeting the congregation, one which is widely useful to anyone moving into a new congregation. She suggests we explore in seven areas—stories and interviews, archived materials, demographics, architecture and visual arts, rituals, events and activities, and people—and ask questions about the congregation's view of God, humanity, nature, time, the church, and Christian mission, and the connections between these. Some practical ways of doing this are the following:

- Inhabit the world of the members of your congregation. It's far more difficult if you are a commuter preacher. Live in the world they live in. This means choosing to live your life in your community, embedding yourself locally: Use local businesses, shop where your members shop (including expeditions to the mall!), walk through the streets and developments, visit the places they work. Not only will you find out about the world they live in, but they will see you in their world. You will be perceived as speaking "as one of us," from within the community rather than pronouncing from outside.
- Discover "memory keepers" in your congregation and community. These are the people who know the stories. You need more than one of them, because each will give you a different perspective. I have had one who was born in the town where the church was, the daughter of a former priest. She grew up there, has never moved more than ten miles away, and was a core member of both the church and the community. Another moved there three years ago, and is immersed in the young family life of the new developments. Another found the church in his retirement, and immersed himself in its life and faith. Together these people knew where skeletons were buried and where plants flourished unexpectedly. They knew the history and the dreams, the values and the blind spots.

• Think about how your church is similar to other churches, and how it is different from them. Some characteristics are true of almost all churches, especially within a denomination—things like liturgy and government. Others are true of some churches but not others—music, socioeconomic status, theological orientation, churchmanship. And there are some things that are unique to a particular congregation—history, personalities, location, relationships, traditions, and stories. And, of course, these last things are most powerful in creating a sense of belonging. Attention to these will create an atmosphere of hospitality in our preaching.

⁓

All this is to say that the effectiveness of preaching in large part depends on the extent to which we mesh our words with the context in which we are preaching. A highly abstract, linguistically rich sermon fits the hallowed arches of St. Alban's Abbey; in the diverse cultures of inner-city Trenton, it is met with incomprehension and boredom. A folksy story with lots of local color tells the deep-rooted generations in rural southern New Jersey that God—and the church—loves them and knows them; in mobile new developments with a three-year turnover, it speaks of an alien world to which they can never belong. It's a question of effective communication: How can we preach so that people can hear us?

But it is also a theological issue. Preaching is about incarnating the gospel, and so is predicated on the incarnation, God made flesh. Christ is the nexus, the point of contact, between God and humanity. When we preach Christ, we do not just repeat his words, simply updated with contemporary language, or retell his story: We re-present Christ himself. If preaching has a sacramental character, then Christ is present in our preaching. If Christ is present in our preaching, then so too is that inherent connection between God and humanity.

Preaching becomes a point where God's world and our world, God's word and our words, connect. It is where all the theory about God becomes real, where we name God active in the everyday stuff of our experience. God is, once again, made flesh.

We need to know the "flesh-world" of our hearers. Who are they? What do they love? What do they fear? What do they do with their time? What are their values, priorities, dreams? These are the things that fill their hearts and minds, the places where they need more than anything to discover the presence of God.

Language

Closely related to our cultural context is the language that we use in our preaching. We often forget the extent to which our language orders our experience—we find it difficult to think, to remember, to imagine, without it. It is how we construe meaning, how we move from sensation to understanding.

Recently I have rediscovered hiking. In the barren shields of Northumbria and Cumbria, on the windswept dunes of the Holy Island of Lindisfarne, I plod one foot at a time. And after a few hours, minutes even, language deserts my brain and my lips. I am alone, exposed, in the presence of God, and it is a wonderful and holy thing. But then I come back, and cannot share that experience. Because language deserted me, I cannot communicate—which is fine for a mystic; not so good for a preacher.

Language is the primary medium of thought and communication, the instrument, the way we know, and so is at the very heart of our preaching. It has the power to create new worlds. Remember how Genesis begins?

> In the beginning when God created the heavens and the earth, the earth was a formless void and darkness covered the face of the deep, while a wind from God swept over the face of the waters. Then God said, "Let there be light"; and there was light. (Genesis 1:1–3)

And in the Gospel of John,

> In the beginning was the Word, and the Word was with God, and the Word was God. He was in the beginning with God. All things came into being through him, and without him not one thing came into being. What has come into being in him was life, and the life was the light of all people. The light shines in the darkness, and the darkness did not overcome it. . . . And the Word became flesh and lived among us, and we have seen his glory, the glory as of a father's only son, full of grace and truth. (John 1:1–5, 14)

Language is at the heart of incarnation, and together language and incarnation are at the heart of preaching. Thus the very words we choose can make all the difference. Words have the power to draw worlds, to reimagine, to shape life as we know it. They are the way we construct meaning and reconstruct it; they are vehicles of grace—and means of hospitality.

Part of what we do—a huge part—as preachers is to invite people into language of faith. To do so, we need to begin with the language they already have. And that means we need to know that language—its vocabulary, its idioms, its references. For many of us, reared in the language of educated faith, we have to learn a second language—or third, or fourth, or fifth. It might be the language of big business or of the factory floor, the language of the playground or the soccer sidelines. We learn these languages in part by simply being with people, spending time with them not only in church but in other contexts as well. We also learn by listening to conversations overheard on trains and in bars; by dragging ourselves away from PBS and NPR to watch and listen to MTV, Fox, and talk radio; and by reading the novels of Oprah's book club and the bestsellers in the airport store, and romances, and magazines.

The next step is to enlarge our hearers' language, to invite them into a richer, deeper linguistic world that will have space in it beyond the ordinary for the extraordinary, the inbreaking, indwelling of God. Language enables us to explore beyond the surface, to evoke the deep memories that connect with our faith. Sometimes this means teaching specific vocabulary, the vocabulary of faith; other times it is a matter of finding words that make the world of God real. Language that is richly descriptive can do this, invoking our senses to connect with images and sound and physicality for the sake of those for whom visual, auditory, and kinesthetic inputs resound above words. Particular phrases can generate feeling, memory, or experience, things like "once upon a time," and even clichés, when used with care and deliberation. This language belongs not just in illustrations and examples, but in talking about and retelling Scripture. It belongs throughout the sermon, as we strive to communicate the word of God. It is the language of imagination, and it allows us to imagine God.

That's the beauty of Eugene Peterson's *The Message*. It's not a translation; it's the story told again in the language of today. It takes its readers out of the realm of "God language" that dates to the seventeenth century, beautiful as it is, to the world of today, where God is not just a historical artifact but a present and active reality. When we use language effectively to create a world and welcome our hearers into it, they will discover, often unexpectedly, that it is their world, and that this God of whom we preach is their God.

OFFERING SPACE

One of the paradoxes of hospitable preaching is that while we may spend many hours honing the content and language of the sermon, in the end what may be more important is what we do not say. Preaching is not simply the transfer of information; rather, it is an event in which people are formed and transformed, not by our words alone but by the working of God in the Holy Spirit. For that to happen, there must be space for our hearers to respond.

Here I would like to distinguish between response and uncritical obedience. Uncritical obedience to a command requires little self-involvement: One is told what to do, and one does it. That immediate, unquestioning action is of crucial importance for soldiers in times of war or when a hurricane is bearing down or a riot threatening. There is no time for discussion, no need for personal investment in the action, or, more importantly, in the principles underlying it; what matters in such a crisis is simply to take the necessary action. But when we preach, we are looking to our hearers to respond with more than mere obedience: We are looking for self-invested, committed response, a response that leaves open the possibility of transformation.

The lives of many of our hearers are essentially passive insofar as they are shaped by predetermined constraints. At work, as economic rationalism gains more influence, we have a job to do. It is a fundamentally utilitarian approach: Everything has a specific purpose, related to the task to be done more than the person who does it. Outside of work, we increasingly spend our time in activities that are either passive—watching TV and movies, going to a sports game, and so on—or programmed—fitness activities, scrapbooking classes, and so on—and require only limited personal investment.

We replicate this in our children. They spend most of their day at school, being taught to the test; outside of school it seems every minute is programmed—soccer, music, homework, dance. Traditional character-building pursuits such as scouting and youth groups are squeezed out in the college-bound resume building, along with time simply to play, time to imagine, time to be re-created.

Strung between a regulated work world and an equally regulated leisure world, we come to church. It doesn't fit in either place—though if pushed, most of our hearers will put it in the leisure category. This is a place where all of us are expected to be active—following our Savior, allowing ourselves to be transformed, making decisions to put our faith into practice.

It's tempting to preach sermons that mimic our culture, that buy into a passive entertainment model. But if we really expect our preaching to be formative and transformative—if we expect anything to actually happen!—then that passive model is inadequate. Our preaching needs to engage our hearers; even more than that, it needs to provide space for them to respond. And providing that space is the work of hospitality.

Perhaps the most profound description of this function of hospitality I have heard comes from Henri J. M. Nouwen:

> Hospitality is not to change people, but to offer them a space where change can take place. . . . The paradox of hospitality is that it wants to create emptiness, not a fearful emptiness but a friendly emptiness where strangers can enter and discover themselves as created free; free to sing their own songs, speak their own languages, dance their own dances; free also to leave and follow their own vocations. Hospitality is not a subtle invitation to adopt the lifestyle of the host, but the gift of a chance for the guests to find their own.[3]

What if we were to substitute the word "preaching" for hospitality"?

> Preaching is not to change people, but to offer them a space where change can take place. . . . The paradox of preaching is that it wants to create emptiness, not a fearful emptiness but a friendly emptiness where strangers can enter and discover themselves as created free; free to sing their own songs, speak their own languages, dance their own dances; free also to leave and follow their own vocations.

Preaching is not a subtle invitation to adopt the lifestyle of the host,
but the gift of a chance for the guests to find their own.

Where I part company from Nouwen is that I am not sure that
preaching—or hospitality for that matter—provides emptiness. The
most spacious places of hospitality are furnished with things that
prompt and invite rest and relationship—full of love, of prayer, of the
Spirit of God, all of which provide companionship in the work of the
soul. Rather, I think of it as a spaciousness that enables freedom.

But Nouwen's vision of the purpose of this space-filled hospitality
is an eloquent description of the role of preaching. Preaching—the
sermon—is not a literary work or a piece of classical music, designed to
be savored, an end in itself. The sermon always looks beyond itself. A
sermon—and I have been guilty of these—from which people depart
saying "what wonderful poetry" has failed, unless it also makes someone
respond "you know, that made me think" or "hmm . . . that made me
want to do something" or "I heard something I needed to hear." Preaching is the word of God calling, hoping, for response.

And that means preaching sermons that invite response in one way
or another, that invite the hearers to take action in their hearts, minds,
souls, lives—to sing, speak, dance, live!

There is no one way to do this. The traditional "come to the altar"
sermon can do it, as can the evocative narrative, the classic three pointer,
and the exploratory inductive. But all must be truly open in what they
offer—real choices.

What our hearers' responses may look like, of course, depends on
both the content and the form of the sermon. When we preach on the
Ten Commandments, a prophetic call to justice, or one of the ethically
hortatory passages of the Pauline epistles, we hope that our hearers will
take note of the (to us) obvious calls to action and respond in practice;
other times we try to tease out the implications of one of Jesus's parables. When we preach a classical evangelistic sermon, we envisage—and
hope for—a response of commitment or recommitment; a sermon on a
psalm of lament might invite a heartfelt sign of recognition: This is how
I feel; maybe God *might* hear me.

Sometimes as preachers we are tempted to manipulate the response, to use the power and authority of our office and our skill with
words to "force" people to respond as we think they need to. I will never

forget the time, relatively early in my ministry, when I looked up during the sermon and saw a number of people in the congregation wiping away tears. At that point I realized the incredible power that a skillful preacher has to awaken emotion, and, at least in those few minutes of a sermon, to determine response. Tears might be evidence of the working of the Holy Spirit; they can also be simple emotional manipulation. We need to stay attentive as preachers in order to discern which is which, and be responsible in our use of words.

And yet there is no question that in many cases it *is* the Holy Spirit that is guiding the response, and so, attentive to this, we do everything we can to make our preaching a space in which the Holy Spirit may work and our hearers can respond. One way to create such a space is through the sermon form or structure.

The reason we think about sermon structure is not to impose some rigid exoskeleton on our preaching but rather, as if creating a map, tracing a route that others can follow. We may know the back roads of our minds, the shortcut dirt tracks and shallow fords and unmarked trails, but others can find it difficult to follow us in those ways. Being aware of sermon form allows us to map out a route that is neither boring nor impossible to follow, which leads people to the glorious vistas without frustrating dead ends. A sermon is like a road trip. We plan it both to maximize our pleasure on the way and to get somewhere in the end. So we need to be clear about both the destination and the route—or else after a first time, no one will be willing to travel along with us.

No one form is inherently more hospitable than another, although some may look more so than others. Human minds function differently. Some of us love to function in the intuitive, abstract space of the mind. For us, inductive sermons are an invitation to play. Others of us relate best to concrete, particular detail; for us, the formal structure of the three-point sermon removes the worry of "where are we going?" and allows us to relax and hear the word of God spoken. Some of us think linearly, and so narrative preaching with its firm hold of plot draws us in; others enjoy the exploratory nature of tangential relationships, and engage most fully with sermons that function that way.

⁓〜

Sermon Structure

The great sermon form of the mid-twentieth century was the *deductive three pointer*: introduction, three major points (or, for that matter, two or four—the number doesn't matter so much as the overall structure), and conclusion. This structure is clear, logical, easy to follow, and easy to remember. It's like inviting people to a home-cooked meal: soup, meat and potatoes, and pies, with maybe a scotch beforehand and coffee afterward. This is simple and sustaining family hospitality at its best.

The introduction sets the scene. It is not primarily designed to get people's attention—they are already a captive audience! Your job here is to make sure you don't lose their attention before you get to the meat of your sermon. So this is a time to tell them why it's worth listening. It is telling people what they should expect and what you are going to do together. Sometimes it might include some background. What we are doing here is setting up the three points, giving the overall theme of the sermon. But this is not the meat of the sermon, and so it should be fairly short.

Then follow the points. These should be clear, memorable, and have some sort of logic that links them. They tend to be propositions, that is, themes or ideas abstracted from your exegetical work; they may (or may not) correspond directly to verses in the scriptural text. Within each point, you want a clear statement of what it is about, and a clear explanation. The way I was taught was fivefold (within each point):

1. State the point.
2. Explain the point.
3. Illustrate the point.
4. Apply the point.
5. Restate the point.

This creates an easy, memorable structure. But you might find that not all of the five are necessary—sometimes your point may be so obvious that it doesn't need a whole lot of illustration, or it may not have an obvious application.

What really matters here is the logic. Your points need to be related in some way. There are a number of different types of logic that can be used to put these three points together. Here are a few of the ways:

- points that correspond with sections of your text
- three aspects of one major theme
- thesis—antithesis—synthesis

Finally, the conclusion should sum up your overall argument, making the logic clear and then telling your congregation what to do in response to what you have said. It need not be long. Traditionally this often included a poem or hymn.

There are a number of questions to ask to see if your sermon is focused and logical:

- Is each point essential to your argument?
- Does it support the main proposition?
- Does the sermon feel balanced? Does each point get about the same amount of attention, or is one significantly more important than the others?
- Is the sermon going anywhere? Is there a sense of climax? Does each point build up the argument?

Although I've called this the three-point sermon, there is no absolute rule that a sermon in this style should have three points. It might have two, or four, or five. The basic structure is the same. But beware if you go over five points—anything that people can't count on the fingers of one hand, they're not likely to remember! Let your form and function guide you, along with your common sense. If you find yourself with more than five points, look to see if some of them are less important, or if you need to preach a second sermon on the same topic to cover all that you want or need to say. Remember that there is no point preaching if your hearers can't absorb what you are saying, so tailor sermons accordingly!

But such meals, eaten night by night without variation, get boring. We are nourished adequately, but after a few weeks of meat and potatoes, we are desperate for takeout, a restaurant dinner, or even just a big bowl of pasta! The three-point sermon is not the only way to preach. In the later twentieth century, a number of other forms came to prominence, and each of them allows us to offer hospitality in a different way. The other extreme from the deductive three-point sermon is the *inductive sermon*. An inductive sermon essentially follows the way we think: It begins at the beginning, and traces the thought pattern of the preacher in preparation. Instead of a rigid exoskeleton, it has a more fluid, exploratory character. We still have a journey and a destination, but it looks more like a meandering country lane than a multilane superhighway.

Fred Craddock, who opened our eyes to this form in his landmark 1971 book, *As One Without Authority*, describes it this way:

> Why not on Sunday morning re-trace the inductive trip [the minister] took earlier and see if his hearers come to that same conclusion? It hardly seems cricket for the minister to have a week's headstart (assuming he studied all week), which puts him psychologically, intellectually, and emotionally so far out front that usually even his introduction is already pregnant with conclusions. It is possible for him to re-create imaginatively the movement of his own thought whereby he came to that conclusion. A second reason for stressing inductive movement in preaching is that if this is done well, one need not often make the applications of the conclusion to the lives of his hearers. If they have made the trip, then it is their conclusion and it is their conclusion and the implication for their own situations are not only clear but personally inescapable. Christian responsibilities are not therefore predicated upon the exhortations of a particular minister (who can be replaced!) but upon the intrinsic force of the hearer's own reflection.[4]

Inductive preaching creates a space in which the hearer is invited to find meaning and to respond.

So how do we do it? By its very nature, inductive preaching is more than a simple matter of rules and techniques—it is an organic form, arising from the preacher's process of reflection on the text. And so in the sermon we will begin at the beginning, face the struggles and problems inherent in our text or theme, and hint at potential resolutions. Inductive preaching is by its very nature inviting. It creates a hospitable space for those who are willing to enter it.

Closely related to inductive preaching is the *narrative sermon*. Story is one of the building blocks of human communication, and so narrative preaching is like inductive preaching insofar as it follows the way we think.

Everybody loves a story. Narrative is exciting: It has movement and action. It is emotionally engaging, involving the whole of our humanity rather than just our minds. Human beings are storytelling creatures; it is how we identify ourselves. It's not surprising, then, that story is one of the ways in which God speaks to us in Scripture, and it was constantly used by Jesus in his teaching. It is a powerful form: Its logic easily overpowers other forms of logic—which is why we often only remember the illustrative stories of a three-point sermon, without remembering the points themselves.

Because narrative is so deeply embedded in our consciousness, it is almost impossible for people not to hear it. It allows us to communicate indirectly, and to provide people space to supply their own interpretations and applications. But because narrative is so powerful, it is easy—intentionally or not—to manipulate people's minds and emotions—so we must be careful how we use it.

But narrative preaching is more than simply telling stories or stringing together illustrations. Few of us want to waste fifteen minutes on a sunny spring morning (or even a snowy winter one) listening to a preacher meander on about pet dogs, golf, or a child's latest "achievement." Eugene Lowry suggests that narrative logic requires conflict and resolution.[5] A crisis is identified and then analyzed in terms of both everyday life and theological dimensions; when things seem to reach rock bottom, resolution is glimpsed; finally, the good news is explored and its consequences for everyday life introduced. It's a pattern that is repeated time and time again in Scripture, for example, in the story of the Annunciation.

There are, of course, other forms of narrative preaching.[6] They include the following:

- pure narrative, telling a story without any commentary, whether it's biblical story, some other story that mirrors the biblical story, or a fictional story inspired by the biblical one. In telling it, it becomes the congregation's story
- juxtaposing a story with Scripture, where Scripture provides the interpretive key to the story without explaining it
- framing a narrative with an introduction and conclusion, putting it in context but without explaining it
- weaving multiple stories together, each interpreting the other(s)

But narrative sermons are not necessarily stories; they may simply follow this logic and include elements of teaching, reflection, illustration, and so on—the same elements as we find in a three-point sermon, but differently arranged. What undergirds narrative preaching is the same as that in all forms of preaching: a theological touchstone.

One final note. Often when well-known narrative preachers are asked to teach narrative preaching, they find themselves at a loss. Narrative preaching is inherently intuitive and resists being overly systematized. Often we may begin at one place and end up somewhere altogether different—and narrative preaching is often the record of that journey. The best way to learn to do it is to journey alongside experienced narrative preachers, to listen and absorb the logic until you feel it in your bones, and then prayerfully to trust God to lead you on a new homiletical journey.

Another form that tends, once again, to be inductive, is a sermon that progresses, as David Buttrick describes it, in a series of *moves*.[7] Each move consists of a discrete idea, scene, or event; the moves are linked by transitions, forming a chain like pearls on a string. Such sermons may have a linear progression, the moves functioning something like stations of a train line. They may be circular, working their way around through a series of tangential relationships in such a way that the hearer's world is expanded. They may be exploratory, like wandering through a garden and stopping to look at and touch and smell particular flowers in order to gain an appreciation of the whole. Or they may be impressionistic, a seemingly random collection of scenes or ideas that, upon stepping back, coalesce to form a whole.

For those of us who operate in a creative, intuitive way, this sermon form is engaging and exciting. However, it also takes skill and discipline, lest it disintegrate into vague ramblings.

If we are serious about preaching hospitably we will use all of these forms—not at the same time!—but across the weeks and months and years of our preaching, so as to offer a welcome to all who hear us.

Returning to Nouwen's exploration of hospitality, we see that while preaching is more about creating space than creating emptiness, the notion of emptiness points us to one crucial thing for encouraging response: the power of disequilibrium.

True hospitality offers comfort; however, monastic hospitality has also always offered discomfort. This is not a place to call home forever, as a guest. One must decide either to join the community, with the duties and obligations that entails, or to move on. Either way, there is a role for hospitable discomfort. Such discomfort, disequilibrium, is the stuff out of which change comes.

For the sermon to prompt response, there must be some point of disequilibrium, some sense of disjunction between where we are now and where we could be, some sense that "things could be different" if only we were willing to take the risk. But the risk is not confined only to the hearers.

RISKING OURSELVES

As preachers, there is always a danger that we will remain detached—the authoritative, disinterested, professional voice—in a conversation in which we expect our hearers to lay themselves on the line, to do that most difficult thing for human beings, to change. So much in the Christian life, and especially in the church, is dependent on relationship. If our hearers sense that we are holding ourselves back, they have every right to do the same.

The Rule of St. Benedict is well aware of the cost of true hospitality. Hospitality cannot be offered without the hosts giving up something of themselves—indeed, provision is made for separate space for them in the community, so that it may maintain the hosts' lives, in recognition that hospitality is a costly intrusion. Hospitality involved not only service provision for the needs of the guest—but presence. Nothing, not even a fast day, is regarded as important as being present to and with a guest. Hospitality is a gift of one's self to the other.

Likewise with preaching. To be effective preachers, to engender that relationship with our congregation that is part of being church, we need to be willing to offer, to risk, ourselves. It's essentially about placing ourselves on the human side of the God-human relationship—we're in it together.

This is part of the power of inductive preaching. It invites our hearers to join us in a journey of discovery—together. But that can be equally true of other sermon forms—it just takes attentiveness to the point of view we project. If we consistently project the image that we are speaking with the voice of God, then while it may engender obedience from some of our hearers, others will react against what they perceive as authoritarianism.[8] By contrast, if we speak from the point of view of the faithful, then we invite them into a conversation of what faithful living might look like.

Of course, all this must be held in tension with the idea that we do, in some real sense, speak with the voice of God. But for us to speak God's voice does not rely on us abrogating our humanity. Rather, as in Christ's incarnation, God chooses to work in and through our created humanity.

All this raises the perennial question of self-revelation in the pulpit—and, more particularly, whether and how often we should use personal illustrations or stories in the pulpit. Some preachers would argue, never—the sermon is about God, not about the preacher. Others would say, frequently—that's how people connect. It all depends on how you understand your role and voice vis-à-vis God's in the preaching event.

Phillips Brooks famously said, "Preaching is truth through personality." We cannot help but reveal ourselves in our preaching. We humans are embodied, and so who we are and what we have experienced will always show in our bodies. Even those who try to erase their personality and experiences from their preaching with a view to "only preaching the word" reveal something about themselves. Thoughtful preachers will be aware of this and, neither ignoring nor playing it up, will allow their bodies and their experiences to become instruments of God's grace.

We have all experienced the power of testimony. One of the main ways we learn is by observing and imitating (or avoiding imitating) others. But the point of speaking from our own experience is not to tell people about ourselves, but to tell them about themselves, to help them recognize themselves in relation to God. Sharing your own experience can be incredibly intimate and vulnerable, speaking out of that deep authenticity that bears witness to a life lived and shaped by encounter with God. But hearers are not our therapists or surgeons—we are not called to bleed all over them. Maintaining our own appropriate boundaries is essential to creating a space for our hearers, to enabling them to meet the living God and respond in faithfulness.

Hospitality is central to our being faithful and effective preachers. It reminds us that our vocation, which we so often experience as a sacred and holy thread that ties us to our God, is in the end not about us at all. It is about the people whom God loves, about creating that place and space of welcome where they may themselves encounter God.

A Wider Circle
A Sermon

Love. Hospitality. Grace. These three words stand out in our first reading. Between them they pretty much capture what this service today, what the ministry of Oasis, is all about. God loves you. You are welcome here. God is gracious.

As I was working on this sermon yesterday afternoon, I thought to myself, "Well, that says it all. God loves you. You are welcome here. God is gracious. A record thirty-second sermon, and we can all go home early."

But it's pretty rare for a preacher to voluntarily give up time in the pulpit, and I'm no exception. So you're stuck with me for the next ten minutes or so, and if you can trust me not to waste your time, I want to share with you a little of what I've been reflecting on this week.

Recently I've been reading a book by a Roman Catholic theologian, James Alison, called *On Being Liked*. There is one chapter that caught my attention straight away and which I keep on returning to time after time after time. The chapter is called "Confessions of a Former Marginaholic." And in it, I recognized myself.

When I was a kid growing up in Australia, I was always the last one to be chosen for sports teams. I did music, I was what was colloquially known as "a brain"—which is not a term of honor in Australian slang—and I didn't like football. I was actually secretly delighted that the team I professed to follow was so firmly at the bottom of the rankings that when I admitted being a Saints supporter, people would look at me with pity in their eyes and kindly change the subject. And I was religious. That was enough to stop any conversations.

And I have to admit that I actually liked it. Once I got over the humiliation of being left out, there was a kind of pride in being different, almost a superiority, because I didn't need *those* people's approval; *I* was being true to myself.

That pattern extended beyond high school. In my evangelical church I was a woman who loved preaching and had this strange idea of being ordained. That cost me most of my friends and eventually my church home. At the evangelical seminary I was not only a woman, but I asked questions and put forward alternative viewpoints, and I was dangerously single. Down the road with the Anglo-catholics, they didn't mind my gender, but now I was too young, still single, and they weren't too sure about what my passion for preaching was all about.

By this time, I was firmly ensconced on the margins, and had come to think of it as a calling, making something holy out of being rejected.

Then I moved to the United States, where the gender and the brain were okay but now I was an immigrant, someone with a strange accent and no history in this place, and still, of course, young, at least in church terms, and still dangerously, ambiguously single.

I still live on the margins. And I sometimes wonder if I am a mar-ginaholic—addicted to this place on the edge. Because it gives me a sense of distinction, a sense of pride. And more than anything else, a sense of identity.

You see, what happens when we feel marginalized, is that we de-fine ourselves as not like "them," whoever "they" might be. It's not sur-prising; it's possibly even inevitable, because that's how we got here in the first place. Someone said, "you don't belong," someone excluded us, someone gave us a label that allowed them to reject us. And, of course, what we do in response is exactly the same. We try to be as little like them as we can, we redefine ourselves to make the differences clear, we make sure there is no confusion, because we have the high moral ground. They drew a circle with us outside. We redrew the circle and left them out.

But in God's eyes there is only one circle, and we are all inside. God loves them. They are welcome. God is gracious. God loves us. We are welcome. God is gracious.

And where that takes us is back to that reading we heard today from 1 Peter. Because if you listened carefully, yes, it was about love and hospitality and grace, but it was actually not about God's love and hos-pitality and grace at all, but ours. We are called to love. We are called to be hospitable. We are called to share God's grace.

I've been thinking a lot about hospitality recently, as part of some writing that I've been doing. Hospitality is a word that is used all over the place. We talk about hotels offering hospitality; we have a hospital-ity room at convention that offers free coffee and snacks; we work on being hospitable at church, which usually means wearing nametags, making sure restrooms are signposted, and seeing that newcomers are invited to coffee hour. But the best definition I've heard was not about the things we do, but something much deeper. Hospitality is an attitude of the heart. It's about being open-hearted.

That's the exact opposite of those circles I was talking about earlier, circles we draw that include some, but inevitably exclude others. Being open-hearted means opening ourselves to others. Not allowing ourselves to draw lines. Being willing to accept them, no matter what they bring.

Most people, when they meet open hearts like these, will respond positively. There's enormous safety in someone who opens their heart to you, who you know will not, cannot, reject you. But the danger of being open-hearted is that some people may meddle with our hearts, maybe even break them.

But if it's hospitality we're called to, if it's love, if it's grace, then that's a risk we may have to take.

As I was writing this sermon yesterday afternoon, I found myself bogged down. I kept writing—and scribbling through—phrases like "I don't like" and "I don't want." Because I don't want to be hospitable if it means it's going to hurt. My hospitable impulse is strong and enthusiastic when I'm being hospitable to people like me, which mostly means people on the margins, one way or another.

But when it's people that are likely to reject me or even attack me, my first impulse is to build up walls of safety, things that will guard my heart and soul. But that's not the way that Christ calls me to. Christ calls me, calls us, to be people of open hearts, open to all.

It's not an easy thing, and I don't want to minimize the cost. To those of us who have been hurt by the church, it may seem too great a thing to ask you to go out to the very people who hurt you and offer your open heart to them. And there are times when for our own survival we can't do it. Those are times to rest in the love and hospitality and grace of others and of our God. But for those of us who can, we're called to risk it all, to keep fighting that impulse to build walls around our hearts and souls, to open our hearts to others, like us or not.

Later in this service we will sing the traditional hymn, "Take my life and let it be." It's a wonderful hymn of offering ourselves, our bodies, souls, and hearts to God and to the work God has called us to.

But I sometimes wonder if the words are so familiar that we don't really "get it" anymore. Sometimes we need to hear the words in another way to really hear them. In their most recent album, U2 sing a song that might just do that. "Take these shoes," they begin, "Click clacking down some dead end street. Take these shoes and make them fit." And as they go on, shoes and shirt and soul and mouth and finally heart, all offered up to Yahweh.[9]

And it says what we barely dare to say. We offer God our hearts knowing that in doing so we offer them to be broken, broken alongside our brokenhearted savior, who loves us, who welcomes us, who offers us his grace.

March 12, 2006—Inaugural service of the Ministry of Oasis in the Diocese of New Jersey
1 Peter 4:7–11
Grace Episcopal Church, Haddonfield, New Jersey

Unexpected
A Sermon

It was a hot day, barely a breath of wind stirring the trees, the sun beating down hard and dust hanging heavy in the air. An ordinary day, by all accounts, marked by nothing more unusual than the unexpected heat. Nothing until the travelers came.

They were unexpected; it was a road not so often traveled, and passersby were few and far between. Down on the plain there were cities and towns, but the people there didn't travel much, except in time of war, especially not up to the heights. But what was strange was that they appeared so suddenly. No telltale cloud of dust appearing on the horizon or down in the valley, no sound of voices carrying through the hot, still air.

But three men, suddenly just a few yards away, three men, strangers, all of them, and seemingly intent on coming his way.

It didn't look like they came for war; there were too few of them and they had no horses or chariots or weapons to attack. But they didn't look familiar either, not members of his far-flung family, or envoys of the city authorities from down on the plain. They were strangers, these men, people he'd never seen before, but it was company, all the same, and that was welcome in this isolated place, and so Abraham struggled to his feet and hurried over to meet them. "My Lord, do not pass by. Stop a while, wash your feet, rest in the shade, eat a little . . . now that you're here."

And so they sat, watching Abraham firing off orders, his wife and servant bustling around making things ready for these unexpected guests. And then they ate, a rich meal of tender veal and local cheese and fresh baked bread.

Abraham still didn't know who they were, still didn't know what they were doing there. He stood awkwardly beside them as they ate, wondering what was going on.

When they finished, they asked a strange question. "Where is Sarah?" Who were these men, who even knew his wife's name? And what did they want with her?

It wasn't until their next words that it finally began to make sense. Kind of. "I will surely return to you in due season," one of the men said, "and your wife Sarah shall have a son."

It was the same thing he had heard from God, the same promise over and over and over again. But a promise that seemed futile. Abraham himself was ninety-nine; his wife wasn't much younger. It couldn't be possible, it just couldn't. And Sarah, Sarah was out the back, listening to the conversation. She heard the men's words and laughed out loud. It was ridiculous. She was well past the age for pregnancy, let alone feeding and changing and sleepless nights. These men were crazy. Their promise was impossible. But still Abraham wondered. These men, they knew Sarah's name? And the promise . . . it was the same one he had heard direct from God: What if it *were* true? How *could* it be? Who were these men?

It's one of those questions that never really gets answered. The way the story is told in the book of Genesis, one moment it's the Lord who is speaking, the next it's the three men. They're human enough to enjoy a good meal, but divine enough to speak on behalf of God. Andrei Rublev's famous fifteenth-century icon, *The Holy Trinity*, which can still be seen in the Tretyakov Gallery in Moscow, depicts the three men as the three persons of the Holy Trinity. Clearly, unequivocably, God. But in Abraham's mind, it seems, it's not quite so clear. What *is* clear is that something quite unexpected, something peculiarly important, has happened. These are no ordinary men; this is no ordinary promise. Abraham's world is about to be decisively changed, changed beyond all recognition, if the promise is to be believed. He might be ready to entertain travelers, but is he ready to entertain God, a God who promises the impossible?

A God who promises the impossible and delivers. Because just three chapters later in the book of Genesis, we read: "The LORD dealt with Sarah as he had said, and the LORD did for Sarah as he had promised. Sarah conceived and bore Abraham a son in his old age, at the time of which God had spoken to him."

When Abraham met those men outside his tent that hot summer day under the oak trees of Mamre, when Abraham met those men, whoever they were, he met God.

That encounter challenged Abraham's ideas of reality, it challenged his common sense. And most of all, it challenged the way he had become accustomed to meeting God. Because up to this point, Abraham's encounters with God had been solitary, mystical affairs. Always, according to the book of Genesis, God could be heard by Abraham alone; often, God's appearance was a visionary event, full of unprecedented commands. "Leave your country; walk through this land; circumcise yourself and your offspring." And the commands were accompanied by promises no less astonishing: "I will give you a land; I will make you a great people; I will establish my covenant with you."

But this time is different. This time the encounter is as simple as offering a meal to some traveling strangers; this time Sarah—and presumably also Abraham's servant—also hear what God has to say; this time, God offers just a promise.

From a solitary, mystical event, Abraham's meeting with God has become a communal, ordinary event—transformed into something extraordinary.

The most ordinary of things transformed. New friends gathered around a plate of meat, some local cheese—the place where God comes with words of blessing.

A piece of bread, a cup of wine—and still God comes with blessing.

It was the memory Jesus left for his disciples the last day of his ordinary human life: a simple meal, bread broken and wine poured, body and blood, and with them his presence for all time.

And still we do this, in remembrance—not just as a way to help remember who this Jesus person was, but expecting, like those first disciples, that we will somehow unaccountably in this simple meal experience Christ's presence, that we will somehow unaccountably encounter God.

But I wonder, are we like Abraham willing to have our world decisively changed, changed beyond all recognition? Are we willing to have God turn our common sense and our preconceptions upside down? Are we willing to let God lead us into a future of new life?

Today we celebrate this community of All Saints here in Bay Head. We celebrate your rector's faithfulness in answering God's call. We celebrate your faithfulness in being willing to stand and work beside him in ministry. And we celebrate the richness of God's promise, made tangible to us in wine and bread. The promise we celebrate is not so much one of words, but the very presence of God with us, the blessing of Christ among us. Christ who is the head of the body, the church, Christ who makes us one.

Today, and every time we celebrate the Eucharist together, we come together not merely to share a meal, but waiting, waiting together for the divine promise, waiting together for the divine blessing, waiting together to encounter God. In that promise and in that blessing, in that encounter with the Holy One, we too will be transformed, transformed from an ordinary bunch of people sharing a simple meal at the Jersey Shore, into the extraordinary people of God.

And we will be strengthened and empowered to do the work of God, to be the face of God in our world.

It was a hot day, and the travelers were unexpected. They ate a simple meal, gave a blessing, and God was there. And nothing would ever be the same again, not for Abraham, not for Sarah, and not for us either. This is just the beginning.

July 18, 2004—Installation of the Rector
Genesis 18:1–10a
All Saints Episcopal Church, Bay Head, New Jersey

NOTES

1. Esther DeWaal, *A Life Giving Way* (London: Geoffrey Chapman, 1995), xviii.

2. This command is so important that it is repeated again and again in Hebrew scripture—a total of thirty-six times according to Rabbi Eliezer W. Gunther Plaut, *Torah: A Modern Commentary* (New York: Union of American Hebrew Congregations, 1979), 1409.

3. Henri Nouwen, *Reaching Out: The Three Movements of the Spiritual Life* (New York: Image Books, 1975), 71–72.

4. Fred B. Craddock, *As One Without Authority*, 3rd ed. (Nashville, TN: Abingdon Press, 1978), 57–58.

5. Eugene Lowry, *The Homiletical Plot: The Sermon as Narrative Art Form* (Atlanta: John Knox Press, 1980).

6. All of which draw on the classic hallmarks of any kind of narrative: plot (sequence, action), character (implicit as well as explicit), setting (time and place, particularity), and point of view (of the storyteller, and hence of the preacher), which any good book on writing will explore in detail.

7. David G. Buttrick, *Homiletic: Moves and Structures* (Philadelphia: Fortress, 1987).

8. Generational theory gives us insights into this: The silent generation tends to respond to authority with obedience; Boomers tend to question authority; Xers tend to demand it be grounded in relationship and authenticity.

9. "Yahweh," from U2, *How to Dismantle an Atomic Bomb*, 2004.

Kingfishers Catch Fire: Play

$\mathcal{O}$ne day when I was five years old, my mother dressed me in one of my father's old business shirts turned back to front and set up a table in the garden. On the table, she placed a jar filled with a runny mixture of flour, water, and food dye, and a large piece of white butcher's paper. I still remember the intense blue of that paint and the wonderful sliminess as it squelched between my fingers. I painted whales.

Recently I went to a conference where time was scheduled each morning before breakfast for spiritual disciplines. As well as continuing our own individual practices, we were given the option of participating in one of two group activities: contemplative morning prayer or another "mystery" offering. The first day, the mystery offering was a walk by the river, paying attention to the richness of God's creation as we experienced it through our senses. The second day we were given paper and a box of watercolors, and invited to paint while someone read the scriptural lessons of the day. I never found out what the mystery offering was for the next day: That second day, on hearing a reference to creation, I found myself absorbed in a series of paintings that occupied me for the remainder of the week. They are not great works of art, but as I placed the paint on the paper, often working it in with my fingers, a new place opened in my soul, a deep connectedness between body and sight and God, not tied to my usual vehicles of thought and word. When I returned home, I scanned the paintings into my computer and created a slide show, a tangible reminder of that holy space.

Paint makes me smile. It awakens in me a playful delight that stretches back into childhood, when blue whales could be painted and flour and food coloring opened a door into imagination, when your whole body could celebrate the wonders of life, and blue paint in your hair and under your fingernails was the sign of holy joy.

⁓⁓⁍

As kingfishers catch fire, dragonflies dráw fláme;
As tumbled over rim in roundy wells
Stones ring; like each tucked string tells, each hung bell's
Bow swung finds tongue to fling out broad its name;
Each mortal thing does one thing and the same:
Deals out that being indoors each one dwells;
Selves—goes itself; myself it speaks and spells,
Crying Whát I do is me: for that I came.

Í say móre: the just man justices;
Kéeps gráce: thát keeps all his goings graces;
Acts in God's eye what in God's eye he is—
Chríst—for Christ plays in ten thousand places,
Lovely in limbs, and lovely in eyes not his
To the Father through the features of men's faces.

—Gerard Manley Hopkins

⁓⁓⁍

Play can connect us with God and with our own selves as God's wondrous creation. It is, for many of us, something that reaches the soul of our humanity. That's important for us as preachers, because without that soul-rootedness, our preaching can become dry and lifeless, a work of the mind rather than of the whole of our God-connected soul. Play engages the whole of our being and allows a whole-personed engagement with God—something that is essential for us as preachers if we are to make connections between the world of God and our world.

Yet as a priest, I find it difficult to play. There is always more work to be done, and guilt weighs heavily if I leave things undone in order to engage in the frivolity of play. I'm on 24/7, at least for emergencies. Being paid a stipend rather than a salary, with no fixed boundaries to my work, no set hours, no physical boundary between the place I live and the place I work, all that means I am always tempted to do more, always feeling guilty that I don't do enough. And because I minister in a small church where the pastor is, structurally speaking, at the heart of everything, it's far too easy to think of myself as indispensable. The nature of priestly life, with its fuzzy boundaries and never-ending list of things to do, makes it difficult for us to justify setting aside, "wasting" time to play. And yet, the aphorism "All work and no play makes Jack a dull boy" is equally applicable to preaching. Without play, my sermons become dry and stale.

Play awakens creativity, it invites delight, it frees my mind to make the often-unexpected connections between the things of God and life around me.

Not long ago at a conference, we were talking about how we go about preparing our sermons. One woman said, "I play Luxor."[1] As some of our group looked on in confusion, others of us joined her in discussing our favorite computer games. Computer games have been my salvation. Shooting colored balls to make a match, clearing rows of symbols by matching colors and shapes, and playing simple card games create a space in which my creative imagination works, where my soul speaks free of the censorship of my mind. The visual, spatial, time-wasting character of the games leaves our unconscious minds open to process what is happening in our souls, and to bring it to birth.

This is no accident. In her useful exploration of the nature of play, psychology professor Catherine Garvey notes that play in children nourishes creativity, problem solving, the development of social roles, identity forming, and language learning.[2] In adults, we see the same processes at work. Play nurtures our creativity, enables us to make connections between language and experience, provides space for unconscious reflection, develops our relationships, and shapes who we are. It is, therefore, an ideal way to nurture our preaching. It nourishes the essential building blocks of our craft; it nourishes our relationships with God.

PLAY IN CHRISTIAN TRADITION

Play is not a prominent theme in Scripture. Check it out in a concordance, and you will find most references are to playing a musical instrument, a few to acting a part, and in 1 Corinthians 10:7–8 it seems to be associated with sexual immorality. Only in Isaiah 11:8 do we find any reference to play as we usually understand it, in the vision of a redeemed world where a child may play without fear of deadly snakes.

Perhaps part of the reason we read so little about play in Scripture is that play is most visible in the lives of children, and in spite of their insatiable appetite for Bible stories, children are not the typical focus of Scripture. From time to time we get glimpses—Joseph, the father's favorite, home while his brothers work the farm; Samuel, awake in the darkness; David slinging stones at Goliath (how much practice must he have had while watching the sheep?). More tantalizing are the apocryphal stories of Jesus in the Infancy Gospel of Thomas, making birds out of clay and setting them free from their dust-bound pallor with a word, gathering water as if it were flowers, playing with other children on a rooftop.[3]

However, for the most part, to find play in Scripture is a work of imagination rather than a careful reading of the text. It's not that the world of Scripture was a world without play; it is simply that play as we know it was not the focus of these writings. We do catch glimpses of playful activity on occasion: David dancing before the Ark of the Covenant in 2 Samuel 6; mouths filled with laughter in Psalm 126; the endless stream of creation, sea monsters, snow, mountains, and creeping things all praising God in Psalm 148. And while the record of Jesus's interaction with children does not go so far as to describe him playing, his use of parables is in itself playful. He invites his hearers to suspend reality for a moment, to enter into an imaginary world that has both continuity and discontinuity with this one. The classic hallmarks of play are here: These parables nourish creativity, problem solving, social roles, identity forming, and language learning. They are pleasurable and spontaneous and require us to "buy in" to catch the meaning. And it is only rarely that Jesus explains his parables; instead, he invites his hearers to explore for themselves. When we hear a parable, we play in that world until we ourselves encounter God and discover that it is not meaning that we were looking for after all, but relationship—with ourselves, with one another, with God.

Scripture speaks to our character as playful beings. The Genesis provision for Sabbath rest, for a time that is inherently nonproductive, makes space for play. When Jesus says, "Consider the lilies of the field," he invites us to a way of being in the world that is totally anchored in the present. Flowers do not work; they are not productive; instead, they reveal their beauty almost absentmindedly.

And play has been present in Christian tradition for many centuries. The pattern of feast days and celebratory fairs in the medieval period ensconced play as analogous to worship—a right sacrifice in honor of the holy one(s). The world was still ordered as work, worship, and rest, but worship encompassed not only liturgical acts but these seasonal rounds of feast days and fairs, from local celebrations to the great St. Bartholomew's Fair.

Originally established as an opportunity to trade cattle and sheep on the Feast of St. Bartholomew and drawing both traders and the pious, wandering minstrels and jesters were also drawn to the scene, and it became more pleasure fair than market. It included such entertainment as loosing live rabbits among the crowds for boys to chase, puppet plays with dual sacred and secular themes, overdressed dolls, and gilt gingerbread. Over the years, however, any semblance of connection with both feast and faith was lost, and by the mid- to late seventeenth century, contemporary accounts report it to have degenerated into licentiousness.

The great mystery plays of the medieval period likewise saw a fusion of faith and play. The players were typically members of craft guilds, who bore the expenses of pageant carts and costumes used to tell the great stories of faith. Cycles of up to forty-eight plays dramatized key biblical stories from creation to the last judgment. And while the original authors were likely clergy with the intent of educating the people, the plays evolved as often raucous entertainment full of humanity and life, echoing the playful illustrations in psalters of this period.

However, the association between play and faith lost ground in the seventeenth through nineteenth centuries. At one extreme, the advent of Puritan simplicity and the Protestant work ethic identified faith with work and decried any frivolous associations; at the other, play became ritualized into formal and too often turgid liturgical pomp and circumstance.

More recently we have seen the reclamation of play for the church in a recognition that children's play is an effective vehicle of faith formation. Not long ago, one of the parents of our Sunday school children, a family new to church, came to me a little confused. "I asked Maddie what she did at Sunday School today," she said, "and she said they played. Didn't she learn anything?"

When Thomas walks into the parish house, finds a prayer book, and heads straight for the altar to play church; when Alex wanders over to the art table and begins an elaborate drawing of himself with his mom and dad and brother and baby Jesus there in the picture beside them because "it's Christmas, you know"; when Alexis and Joshua sing the Taizé chant "Eat this Bread" on road trips; when Sarah stands by the font with a baby doll in her arms and Luke pours water on the baby's head, then you know that they have played their way into God's world, that their imaginations have become suffused with the glory of God. Because for them, God is not only interested in religion, but pervades every inch of their being and living, and play is the place where that deep confidence is expressed, where they delight in that all-pervasive holy presence.

But most adults have lost the capacity for instinctive faith play. Years of being told that church was for adults and they had better behave, of stern looks and prods in the back from grumpy parishioners, of being relegated to the nursery—as young children and then as teenagers assigned to nursery duty—have convinced us that play and church are worlds far apart. Things have begun to change in many churches, but the legacy of the stern experiences of our childhood has firmly convinced us that God doesn't want us to play. We are serious and committed in our faith, not frivolous flibbertigibbets.

As preachers, however, we need the life that play can bring us. If Garvey is right, and play is essential for creativity and so on, and if play enables us to engage with the holy, it is an essential part of our spiritual preparation.

HOW DOES PLAY WORK?

Play takes us to the edge. When we play, we step outside our normal roles and structures, and engage differently with the world. Play allows us to see new possibilities, new relationships, that we could have never imagined in our ordinary structured world. But it is precisely these possibilities, these relationships, that form the heart of preaching as we make connections between God's world and our world.

This sense of play taking us to the edge is perhaps most usefully explored using the work of Victor Turner on liminality.[4] Turner describes liminality as structured ambiguity, the period of social limbo that occurs when we step outside the structural world as we ordinarily know it into a space apart. Liminality happens when we let go of the roles, constraints, and expectations of everyday life and allow ourselves to enter a space of freedom.

The Merriam-Webster's dictionary defines "liminal" as "of, relating to, or being an intermediate state, phase, or condition." Liminality happens when we are on the margins. It happens whenever structure does not dominate our lives. It is here that innovation occurs, innovation that is later cemented in structure. What this means is that when we play, creative connections form, often unconsciously, that link our world and God's. We take those connections and incorporate them into the form that we call "sermon."

We experience liminality most often when we are in some form of transition. In its negative form, it happens when we leave one job and wait to begin another, when we leave one home and have not quite established another. For clergy, it often occurs when we know/discern that it is time to leave our current ministry, but a future ministry has not yet opened up for us, that interminable period when search committees visit and we imagine ourselves in another context, yet still have to get on with burying parishioners and planning Sunday school and scheduling weddings. Such liminality can be a time of impatience, and yet at the same time a time of growth and creativity, albeit often unconscious. Liminality is that time of late pregnancy, knowing a child is growing within you, when everything you see seems shot through with significance and promise, when earth is pervaded by the glory of God. It is these times when for no apparent reasons everything sharpens into focus, and you want to shout to the world, "Don't you see it?"

Another place where liminality is often experienced is in worship. Turner focuses on the liminal nature of ritual in which the participants are freed from social structures, existing in a time and world apart. This is when, from a Christian point of view, we join our voices with all the company of heaven, saying "Holy, Holy, Holy Lord." In such a context, life opens up into possibility. We are freed to express ourselves fully, with all our hopes and fears and dreams, to reflect on meaning, to imagine what could be. Such an experience makes transformation possible.

Worship and ritual can be powerful liminal experiences, but for us as preachers, we are so often absorbed in engineering that space for others that we are not free to experience it for ourselves. The relentlessness of ritual, the spaciousness of prayer, the freedom of letting oneself drift in the ebb and flow of glory—from the pew, at its best, it is liminal. But from the pulpit and altar, it is constant worrying whether the next reader will show, and counting heads to work out how much bread to consecrate, and trying not to forget the three prayer requests made while you were standing in the narthex waiting to process in, and trying to intercept the glare of a mother whose acolyte son is fidgeting, and ignoring the prickly trickle of sweat down your back. Far from being released from structure, we are at our most confined, bound into role and expectation both by our church structures and by the simple fact that worship is our job. And so the occasions are rare—albeit wonderful—when we break through into that state.

But liminal experience is not restricted to worship. In fact, as Turner identified in the title of his seminal book on liminality, ritual and liturgy are themselves a form of play, albeit one that is highly structured. In play, we so often worship. We, the functionaries of liturgy, are finally able to celebrate, to give ourselves over, to lose ourselves in the glory of creation, of the incarnation, to hear the Spirit speak our names.

Play and worship are integrally intertwined, if not by experience, then by effect. Guardini said that worship is wasting time for God; in like manner, play is joining God in the sabbatical seventh-day rest, a time to delight in all that God has made, including our own selves, and in God.

When we play, we enter that magical space where time becomes malleable and place translucent. We lose ourselves in an experience that is fully anchored in the present, stepping aside from our past and delaying entering our future. This type of experience is described by Victor Turner as a liminal one, that in-between space that is "an instant of pure potentiality, when everything, as it were, trembles in the balance."[5] It is a moment of freedom.

If play brings us into a liminal space, then it opens and frees us so that we can imagine new ways of doing things, explore alternative interpretations, reenvision the world. And, more radically, it opens us to the Spirit of God. Why? Because at the heart of our faith is the notion that with faith goes transformation. "Behold, I make all things new," says the voice of the Lord in Isaiah. "And I saw a new heaven and a new earth," says John in Revelation.

And this is where play connects with preaching. Turner argues that "liminality, marginality, and structural inferiority are conditions in which are frequently generated myths, symbols, rituals, philosophical systems, and works of art."[6] In other words, liminality, that structural state of ambiguity, feeds creativity. It helps us to make those unexpected connections, those spirited leaps of the imagination, that bring God's word to life in our lives.

Most preachers have experienced this at some time or other. We've meditated on the text, analyzed it with the help of commentaries, and explored how others have interpreted it; we've thought about our congregation and context. And then we get stuck. Nothing seems to be worth saying. And so we put our work aside and go for a walk or take a nap or spend time with our children. And somehow, unaccountably, the way forward seems crystal clear, and we can barely write fast enough to get the ideas down. It's as if God finally deigned to show up—or perhaps that we were at last open enough for the Spirit to do its work.

Why is this? Precisely because activities that are liminal in character, by definition, are not part of the ordinary structures of society. When we engage in liminal activities, we are freed up to seek out alternative structures, those which are ordinarily inaccessible or simply hidden to ordinary sight and understanding. Liminality is going into the wilderness and discovering what God has for us there; it is that heightened sense of everything that comes when we are attentive in the margins, when we experience ambiguity as blessing and liberation. We see things from a new perspective, a perspective that, because it is not inherently linked to the normal, allows us to see things we would otherwise miss. And these include the things of God.

Or, at least, that is its potential. We all know people whose response to the liminal is to leap as fast as they can back into the safety and security of structure, never allowing themselves the gift of exploring potential alternatives. The freedom liminality offers is, for most of us, tremendously unsettling. None of the props that we ordinarily rely on, the things that support our identity, are present. It is perhaps why, when my diocese offered a beach day as part of our clergy continuing-education program, few attended. The idea of a day in the sun and sand, playing beach volleyball, hanging out by the grill, enjoying friendships and conversation, was too threatening. Liminal spaces often feel dangerous.

But dangerous spaces are often where we find God. When Moses stood by a bush that burned without turning to ash, when Job raged at the whirlwind, when Paul stumbled under a blinding light, they met God. Their lives were forever changed. It's just as C. S. Lewis said in that wonderful conversation between the children and Mr. and Mrs. Beaver:

> "Is [Aslan]—quite safe? I shall feel rather nervous about meeting a lion." "That you will, dearie, and no mistake," said Mrs. Beaver; "if there's anyone who can appear before Aslan without their knees knocking, they're either braver than most or else just silly."
>
> "Then he isn't safe?" said Lucy. "Safe?" said Mr. Beaver; "don't you hear what Mrs. Beaver tells you? Who said anything about safe? 'Course he isn't safe. But he's good. He's the King, I tell you."[7]

Safety, or the Spirit of God? Dare we take the risk and open ourselves in play?

BEGINNING TO PLAY

Play is wonderful. But while there are endless books on traditional spiritual disciplines, books on how to play are few and far between. I suspect that's because they are, fundamentally, redundant. If we're going to enter that liminal space we call play, then manuals creating playful structure are self-defeating. Most sensible would be to simply say, as we do to children, "Go outside and play!"

A story is told of the great nineteenth-century preacher, Phillips Brooks (1835–1893), perhaps best known for his hymn, "O Little Town of Bethlehem." He was a reserved and earnest man, who followed a rigorous weekly structure of sermon preparation. But every Saturday afternoon, his final sermon text settled, he would wander the streets of Boston window-shopping, visit his friends, and play with their children. His early biographer and acquaintance William Lawrence writes of him,

> Perhaps his most charming trait was his love of children. There was no suggestion of fear on their part; he was one of them, as cheery, simple and unconscious. I have seen him dart away from a company

of clergymen and others on the piazza, march out upon the lawn, and with a child's trumpet lead the regiment around and around, with no thought of anything but the game.[8]

Another biographer writes of Brooks' visits to families,

> He would incite, or seem to do so, the children to disobedience, as though law and order in the household were a sham; like some picture from *Alice of Wonderland*, where things were reversed or lost their normal relations. To considerations of personal dignity of bearing he would become oblivious, romping on the floor or standing as Goliath for some small David of a boy to use his sling.[9]

It's hardly the typical image of a famous preacher, a 6'4" three-hundred-pound man crawling around the floor with kids. Yet it was an essential part of his humanity, an essential part of his preparation to preach. And Phillips Brooks was not alone. Barbara Brown Taylor writes of watching movies, reading poetry, rearranging hay in the hayloft, and taking long walks as she prepares her sermons.[10] Play—in whatever form it takes—becomes a crucial element in the creative process.

However, those of us who have gotten out of the habit of playing may need some help. So let's begin with a definition of play. Catherine Garvey's is as useful as any. She defines it as follows:

1. Play is pleasurable, enjoyable. Even when not actually accompanied by signs of mirth, it is still positively valued by the player.
2. Play has no extrinsic goals. Its motivators are intrinsic and serve no other objectives. In fact, it is more an enjoyment of means than an effort devoted to some particular end. In utilitarian terms, it is inherently unproductive.
3. Play is spontaneous and voluntary. It is not obligatory but is freely chosen by the player.
4. Play involves some active engagement in the part of the player.[11]

It's simple really. Find something you enjoy doing, something that gives you pleasure. And do it. Don't get too caught up in it being the perfect match for the definition: that's just a place to begin. Play is activity free of "shoulds." Sometimes it has a productive side to it—building relationships, tending the garden, getting fitter. But they are simply byproducts. What matters is the delight, the spontaneity, the transformation of our ordinary lives. Play offers us the loss of inhibition without the side effects of alcohol or drugs. It's when you let the fields lie fallow, and they surprise you with a profusion of wildflowers (and everyone knows that wildflowers make the best sermons!). It's where the unexpected comes to life.

Dave Barry catches the character of play in a recent review in the *New York Times*:

> I have often been accused of slacking. When I wrote a weekly humor column, people were always saying to me, "So . . . you write one column a week?" They wouldn't come right out and say the rest of what they were thinking, which was: "And how long does that take you? Two hours a week?" But I knew.
>
> What these people failed to understand is that the hard part of writing is not the typing part, but the thinking part. If you were to come into my office, you would most likely see me engaged in some activity that did not appear, to your untrained eye, to be work. You might see me clipping my toenails, or exploring the vast information resources of the Internet, such as the site that tells you what song was No. 1 on the record charts on any given day for the past 60 years. Or you might see me thrashing around with my electric guitar in my futile but ongoing (for nearly four decades) attempt to learn the guitar part to "Paperback Writer," which was No. 1 on my 19th birthday.
>
> You'd probably think I was slacking. But you would be wrong. Because while I am engaged in these seemingly pointless activities, I am thinking about a critical writing issue, such as: Which is a funnier-sounding mineral name, feldspar or potash? It takes hours of grueling mental effort to solve that kind of problem, but you, the reader, see only the finished product (feldspar).[12]

It's the same for preachers.

Play is the field of the imagination, the realization of the impossible. The ways we play are endless, and deeply personal. I've learned a lot about play from watching my cat, Bede. He has a beloved toy. It is a wombat—in real life a furry Australian marsupial about the size and shape of a short-legged pig with a face something like a rabbit who has run into a wall; Bede's wombat is much smaller, about six inches long and four in diameter, with stubby legs and a plastic nose and eyes. Sometimes I wake at nights to the sound of something soft hitting the vinyl floor. It is the wombat. Bede grabs it in his mouth and tosses it in the air . . . and then leaps after it, twisting and turning in the air in his attempt to catch it as it falls. I can only assume that Bede thinks that he is hunting; what strikes me in those moments is his pure, unalloyed joy, and the lithe grace of this small creature. He is playing.

The closest I can get to that feeling is when I grab my boogie board and catch a decent-sized wave. There is a rush of pure pleasure and the sense of being caught up in something much more powerful than myself (albeit ending with the inevitable scraping across gravelly sand or, on more dramatic occasions, the snap of my Styrofoam board as I am dumped unceremoniously on the beach). Or the unexpected buoyancy as I drop my pack after a three-mile climb, my passage documented in photographs: a turtle looking anxiously at me from the middle of the trail, his head half-withdrawn on leathery neck into his carapace; a caterpillar, hanging from a thread in the woods; a tumble of rocks both solid and fragmentary; water rippling over stones.

At the core of our play is finding that which feeds our souls, that which invites us to experience God. For me it's nature—most often at its wildest—and children. I take joy in the little girl who bends double in front of the altar to pick up sequins fallen from Easter banners, in hanging out by the pool with families, in reading bedtime stories to small new parishioners, and in holding tiny babies close, resting in our mutual contented safety.

PLAY AND SABBATH

And on the seventh day God finished the work that he had done, and he rested on the seventh day from all the work that he had done. So God blessed the seventh day and hallowed it, because on it God rested from all the work that he had done in creation. (Genesis 2:2–3)

The Sabbath in Jewish tradition is a time for rest from creation, a time to set one's daily life aside and turn to God. It is a time when time itself almost ceases to exist, from sundown to sundown measured only by the passage of moon and sun.

There is immense freedom in such a time. It removes us from that compulsion to produce and consume that defines so much of who we are; barricades of ritual proclaim it a place of safety. It puts a new rhythm in place, one not constricted by the hours of work and household, but by rest and worship, a time to remember who we are and who God is.

Yet there is a danger residual in this traditional Sabbath definition. I remember hearing the story of someone's Jewish grandmother who observed Sabbath rigorously. She would not even turn on a light switch—that was work. Because she was frail and didn't see too well, she spent her Sabbath days sitting in darkness, afraid to move, unable to see. But it's not confined to Judaism; Christian sabbatarianism dragged generations away from the church with its insistence on tediously long services and endless dull afternoons devoid of story and play. Sabbath became a prison, rather than an occasion for delight in God. No wonder Jesus said, "The Sabbath was made for humankind, and not humankind for the Sabbath."

That's the negative side of Sabbath, the soul- and faith-destroying one. But it doesn't have to be like that. In her book on spiritual practice, *Mudhouse Sabbath*, Lauren Winner writes of her yearning for Sabbath after her conversion from Judaism to Christianity, remembering the blessedness of that time apart. She points the reader to this description by Nan Fink: "Shabbat is like nothing else. Time as we know it does not exist for these twenty-four hours, and the worries of the week soon fall away. A feeling of joy appears. The smallest object, a leaf or a spoon, shimmers in a soft light, and the heart opens. Shabbat is a meditation of unbelievable beauty."[13]

Perhaps what we need to do, to escape from the deadening associations of rules and regulations, is to reclaim the Christian Sabbath, not as the sixteenth- and seventeenth-century Puritans did, legislating "holiness" on Sundays, but rather reclaiming the essence as it was practiced by the early Christians. They kept Sabbath, a day of sacred stillness that echoed the rest of the Creator, and they kept a new holy day, Sunday, a day of creative holy activity: time to pray, and time to play.

A convent that I used to visit had a unique interpretation of Sabbath. Every so often, they would gift one of their community with a "should-free" day. On that day, that person was totally free to do whatever they wished—there were no rules, no boundaries, no limits.

At certain times in my life, I have tried the "should-free" version of Sabbath. I have eaten ice cream for breakfast, cooked gourmet meals, and sat on the porch and watched squirrels. I watched turtles sunning themselves on semi-submerged logs, and the dark diamond shadows of fish in a canal. Time lost its dominion. I found myself absent-mindedly turning to God.

Sabbath is so much more than a set of rules. It is putting aside the things that demand our attention and allowing our minds and bodies to relax into the present. We are free to live not where we have been or where we are going, but simply where we are, surrounded by God's grace. And then we can allow our attention to be caught by the things that delight us.

In play, we delight in God's creation. In play, we engage in God's re-creation. In play, we approach the holy. Play is essential in the re-creation of our hearts and souls. It opens a space that is free to explore, to imagine, to dream, to believe, a space where we may indeed encounter God. Play is something in which we both lose and find ourselves. And the spontaneity it engenders comes with us when we approach the text. Play enables us to experience the freedom intended by God, as we delight with unconscious consciousness in God, a delight that brings life to our preaching.

A Deep Breath

A Sermon

There are some stories that I just love to hear read in our churches. And one of them is our Gospel for today. You probably haven't heard it before: It used to be that we would read the bit about Jairus and his daughter, but leave out the bit about the woman with a hemorrhage.

I'm not sure why they left it out: perhaps because they thought it was the kind of women's business which is generally regarded as unmentionable in polite company, perhaps just because it made the reading awfully long.

But either way, we really missed out. Not just on the story itself, though that is bad enough, but on the way it fits in with the rest of what is going on.

Jesus is busy, there's no doubt about that. The public ministry that began with his baptism in the Jordan and ended with his death is in full swing.

He's preaching, teaching, and working miracles, and the towns and villages are buzzing with the question, Who is this man?

They asked it in our reading last week, when he calmed the wind and the waves; they'll ask it again next week, when he goes back to his hometown. But this week, it is Jesus who is asking the questions, and in their answers, the people themselves tell us who he is.

It all begins when Jesus gets back into his boat, turns around, and heads back to the other shore. This time there are no waves, no storm, just a regular crossing, worthy of no special attention. He lands, and immediately people crowd around him, struggling to be heard.

A man pushes his way through, wealthy, by the looks of him, a leader. Not the sort of person you'd expect to come to see a wandering preacher. But he is at his wit's end. And so he comes, this man Jairus, falling down in front of Jesus, begging him to come and save the most important thing in his life—his daughter—because his daughter is dying, and there is nothing more that he, or the doctors, or the religious leaders, or anyone else can do. So he begs Jesus just to come and lay hands on her, and maybe, maybe, she will live. And Jesus takes pity on him, and begins to follow him.

But suddenly, he stops. "Who touched me?" he said. "Who touched me?" And there are people everywhere, crowding in on every side. It is a ridiculous question. No one could know who bumped into him. And his disciples tell him so. "You can see the crowd. Anyone could have touched you. What are you fussing about?" And Jairus most likely tries to distract him, to hurry him on in time to save his little girl. "Hurry, hurry, my daughter is dying!" But Jesus just stands there. "Who touched me?"

And then a woman comes forward, just the opposite of the man Jairus. She looks worn, tired; where he expected people to make room for him, she seems to almost shrink into the ground. "It was me," she says. "I didn't think it would do any harm. But it's been so many years. I just thought that if I touched you, just the edge of your clothes, maybe the bleeding would stop, maybe I would be well again. I didn't think it would matter." Jesus looks at her and said, "Daughter, your faith has made you well. Go in peace."

But it's too late. Some messengers arrive. They have bad news. While Jesus has been fussing about who touched him, the worst has happened. The little girl has died. They tell Jairus to stop bothering Jesus and go home to mourn.

And everyone wonders, What if?

What if that woman hadn't bothered Jesus? What if he had hurried on? Did that little girl die all because of an impatient woman?

But there's no time for speculation. Jesus overhears them. "Do not fear, only believe." And he grabs three of his closest followers, and they head toward the house where the little girl's body lies.

When they get there, people are standing round crying, absolutely heartbroken. Jesus looks at them, and they cannot believe what he says. Doesn't he have a heart?

They have seen her body, they know what death looks like, and here he is, making fun of them. "Why are you weeping? She's not dead, only sleeping." Their tears turn to hysteria.

And he goes into the house, and sends everyone away, even her parents, puts her hand in his, and says, "*Talitha cum*. Little girl, get up." And the dead child wakes up, and walks out to her parents, and Jesus tells them to get her something to eat.

The story ends well, like all good stories. But some pretty disturbing stuff remains. I mean, how could Jesus do that? How could he let the family go through it all? Didn't he have any idea what it would be like to lose a child? What was he thinking? Surely the woman could have waited, surely he could have brushed her aside and dealt with her later? Surely that's not too much for the Son of God?

Yet, there is something very powerful about Jesus's actions in this story. We live in a world where there are more and more demands on us every day. If your life is anything like mine, there are times when I feel like I'm being buried under its weight. Summer offers a little bit of a letup, at least in theory, but in practice it seems to be just as busy, just with different things.

We spend our lives prioritizing, rushing through things or doing them halfway because we can't quite get them done, skipping out on the things that are important for the long term so that we can get the stuff done that was on our agenda for yesterday. We try to make judgments about what is most important, and the things that are less important get relegated to second or, perhaps more often, last place. Sometimes, in doing that, we miss things we should have done. We all know how it happens. The urgent overwhelms the important. We even have proverbs to describe what happens, things like "The squeaky wheel gets the oil."

But sometimes, in responding to the urgent, we forget what is important. We eat fast food because we ran out of time to do the shopping. We put off going to the doctor because our calendar has gotten too full. We cut our hours of sleep, and then wonder why our energy has disappeared. Our weekly phone call to our parents or children becomes every second week, then every month, because we couldn't work out how to fit it in. We can't take a vacation, because we couldn't find the time to plan. We forget to pray, because there is just too much else going on in our busy minds.

As you might have guessed, this is an issue for me. Me, and probably 90 percent of the population. In the end, we don't do what is really important. We don't do the things that will make a difference to our lives, now and in the future, the things that will make a difference to those in need, the things that will make a difference in the world.

It almost seems a trivial thing to draw from our Gospel today. After all, Jesus was dealing with matters of life and death with the little girl. Surely, the woman could have waited. Or maybe not. You see, she'd been bleeding for twelve years. That meant, under the religious law of the time, that she was unclean. She couldn't go near anyone, she couldn't worship, she couldn't work. Anything she touched would be unclean. It was a life of total, unimaginable isolation. She might as well be dead.

And in that one act she took a chance. Took a chance, perhaps her last chance to reenter the land of the living.

And if Jesus hadn't stopped, hadn't asked who she was, who knows what would have happened. It might have been her last chance at faith, her last chance at life.

Of course Jesus, unlike us, was able to go on, and raise the little girl as well. We can't depend on that. But the story is significant enough to make me ask: What if I just did do what is necessary, if I paid more attention to what is here and now and less to what is calling from a distance? What difference would it make in my life? What about in someone else's life?

A traditional part of many spiritual practices is the discipline of being attentive: watching the world around you, listening carefully, seeing what really needs doing, and what, perhaps, can be left for another day.

This summer, take a deep breath. Look around. See what God is calling you to. Some of it may be the mundane, the quiet, the everyday. Some of it may be taking care of yourself, your relationships with others, your relationship with God. Pay attention, and allow God to guide you out of busyness into the sort of open and responsive life that we see so clearly in Jesus Christ.

June 29, 2003—Proper 8, Year B
Mark 5:21–43
Trinity Episcopal "Old Swedes" Church, Swedesboro, New Jersey

The Wall

A Sermon

The wall is high, almost as high as you can see. It is made of grayish-colored stone, granite maybe, with streaks of brown here and there and glints of shiny mica. The stones are rough cut, but fitted together better than a child's building bricks. The cracks are filled with smaller stones, and sand and mud, and green slime in the perpetually damp places. And when you rub the stones with your finger, it comes away black with the grime of centuries. Over it all grow mosses in the cracks that reach deep inside, and ivy and honeysuckle wind around, veiling the surface and creating the illusion of a living creature.

But it is dead, long dead. The organisms that had been part of the making of that stone are long gone, and gone as well are the people who built the wall, stone by careful stone. It still stands firm, no chance of being moved; built long before your lifetime, long before even living memory, and it is sure to outlive even you, and your children, and your children's children. That big old wall is here to stay.

But on the other side, on the other side, is just one of those places you have to go. One of those places that has a "keep out" sign strung across it that makes every ten-year-old boy want to go there all the more. This time the sign is just that massive pile of stone, but the message is still clear. This is one big barrier, and you're not invited in.

Not that you don't try. You find a nice thick stem of ivy and wrap it round your hand; you wedge your toe into a crack, and begin to climb. But you're barely three feet off the ground when that nice thick stem of ivy gives way, and you're flat on your back on the ground.

So you try a different way. This is the spider method. You lie flat against the honeysuckle and kind of wind yourself in among it, and edge your way up, one foot, two feet, three—it's going better this time—four, five. . . . And then the little loops under your feet begin to tear, and you slide back down to where you began.

Okay, this isn't working.

You begin to think of other alternatives. Maybe you could find a friend, climb up on their back, balance on their shoulders, all to see if you can get a hold of the top of the wall to swing yourself over. But there's no guarantee, when you get as high as you can, that you won't still find wall above you, and no other way of getting up there. Or maybe a ladder, one of those big, tall ones used to clean windows or maybe even one of those magical extending ones that lives on a fire truck. Or a rope, looped somehow over the top, so you can pull yourself up.

But looking around, there's no ladder, no rope, least of all a friend. Surely there is some way to get to the other side of that wall?

But maybe, you think, maybe there's an end to it, maybe there's another way in. So you head off to explore. One, two, three, four . . . you decide to count your paces . . . fifty-seven, fifty-eight . . . one hundred and seventy-three, one hundred and seventy-four, one hundred and seventy-five . . . three hundred and nineteen, six hundred and thirty-one. . . .

Your feet are getting sore. It feels like there is a blister on your left heel, and maybe one beginning on your right big toe as well. One thousand, two hundred and eighty-six, one thousand, two hundred and eighty-seven, one thousand, two hundred and eighty-eight. Two hours later, the wall is still there, and your legs hurt. The honeysuckle and ivy have disappeared and then grown again. A little ways back you saw some roses, but most of the time it has been just hard, gray stone. There's no sign of an end to it. Just as high as it ever was, it reaches back into the distance, and far away ahead as the horizon. You've lost count of your steps, it makes no sense to count anymore, it doesn't really matter, except that if you want to go back to where you began, it's the only way to measure how far. The wall looks pretty much the same all the way so far.

You decide to go just a little farther, just in case that last effort brings you to the end, or maybe, just maybe, to a gate, a door, into the hidden place. Because as tired as you are, as ready to give up, there is a piece of you that thinks that whatever is behind there really must be worth seeing, to have this much protection around it, whatever is behind is worth almost anything that it could cost.

And so you plod on. Left foot, right foot, left foot, right foot, left foot . . . until your feet simply refuse to go any further. You give up, and collapse on the ground, back against the wall, your muscles protesting loudly, wishing you had a long drink of water—anything cool to wash the taste of stone dust out of your mouth.

You feel afraid, afraid that you'll be trapped here forever, walking alongside this old stone wall, never catching even a glimpse of what is on the other side. Is this all that life will amount to? You think back over the last few hours, days, months, what you have done, what you have left undone. The mistakes you've made. The things you've got right. The wrongs done to you. The unexpected gifts. The people you have hurt. The ones you've loved. All these things swirl around in your mind, one after the other after the other, round and round and round. And you give up on finding whatever is on the other side of the wall. There is nothing more you can do.

And then from behind your back, you begin to hear a noise, the grind of stone shifting, the unexpected pressure of stones against your back.

The noise grows, and you jump way from the wall, just in time to see puffs of dust from along the top—you can see it now—and the rumble like thunder.

And then it begins to crumble, almost silently it seems, blue sky appearing between the shifting stones, and the top sags and bends, until suddenly it comes down with a crash!

And on the other side, through the dust and rubble, you see something that looks like a person. Something tall and kind of shining white.

As the dust clears, you see it is a man, a man like no other, with arms stretched out to greet you, and with holes in the palms of his hands.

No longer tired, no longer afraid, you begin to climb over the rubble to meet your Savior.

"Therefore, my friends, since we have confidence to enter the sanctuary by the blood of Jesus, by the new and living way that he opened for us through the curtain (that is, through his flesh), and since we have a great priest over the house of God, let us approach with a true heart in full assurance of faith, with our hearts sprinkled clean from an evil conscience and our bodies washed with pure water. Let us hold fast to the confession of our hope without wavering, for he who has promised is faithful. And let us consider how to provoke one another to love and good deeds, not neglecting to meet together, as is the habit of some, but encouraging one another, and all the more as you see the Day approaching" (Hebrews 10:19–25).

Sunday, November 16, 2003—Proper 28, Year B
Hebrews 10:11–25
Trinity Episcopal "Old Swedes" Church, Swedesboro, New Jersey

NOTES

1. A game where you destroy serpentine lines of balls by shooting matching colored balls at them.

2. Catherine Garvey, *Play,* enlarged edition (Cambridge: Harvard University Press, 1990), 5.

3. Although not all the stories are as attractive: In the Infancy Gospel, Jesus often appears a petulant and vindictive child, cursing those who offend him.

4. Most useful in this respect is Victor Turner, *From Ritual to Theatre: The Human Seriousness of Play* (New York: Performing Arts Journal Publications, 1982).

5. Turner, *From Ritual to Theatre*, 44.

6. Victor Turner, *The Ritual Process: Structure and Anti-Structure* (Chicago: Aldine Publishing, 1969), 128.

7. C. S. Lewis, *The Lion, the Witch and the Wardrobe* (New York: Harper Trophy, 1950), 80.

8. William Lawrence, *A Life of Phillips Brooks* (New York: Harper and Brother, 1930), 122.

9. Alexander V. G. Allen, *Phillips Brooks 1835–1893: Memoirs of His Life with Extracts from His Letters and Notebooks* (New York: E. P. Dutton and Company, 1907), 568.

10. Barbara Brown Taylor, in *Birthing the Sermon: Women Preachers on the Creative Process*, ed. Jana Childers (St. Louis, MO: Chalice Press, 2001), 156.

11. Garvey, *Play*, 4.

12. Dave Barry, review of *Doing Nothing: A History of Loafers, Loungers, Slackers, and Bums in America*, by Tom Lutz, *New York Times Book Review*, June 5, 2006, 11.

13. Nan Fink, *Stranger in the Midst: A Memoir of Spiritual Discovery* (New York: Basic Books, 1997), 96.

· 6 ·

Holy Conversation: Prayer

*R*ecently I went on retreat at a monastery. The days were defined by prayer: Morning Prayer at 6:00 am, Eucharist at 7:45 am, Midday Prayer at 12:30 pm, Evening Prayer at 6:00 pm, and Compline at 8:30 pm. In the chapel, the light stained blue by the windows, the lingering smell of incense perfuming my breath, the droplets of water reminding me of baptism, the lull of voices in quiet harmony, and the honeyed taste of fresh baked bread all served to invite me into prayer. Apart from the insistent call of the alarm clock while it was still dark, praying was easy. It came naturally.

But few of us live in monasteries or other Christian communities. We can't rely on others to make sure that we pray. Whatever we expect our prayer life to look like, we have to make it happen ourselves. And as preachers, it's essential: Our relationship with God, fed and strengthened in prayer, is what makes it possible to preach with authenticity.

Episcopalians have a tradition of daily prayer, morning and evening, known as the daily office. That's the tradition; the reality is that it is offered as a public service in very few places, and in even fewer of those is the offer taken up by the congregation. For two years in my first solo parish, I advertised morning prayer at 8:30 am Monday through Thursday; I can count on the fingers of one hand the parishioners who joined me. Maybe it was the time, though I would happily have changed it had there been any interest; maybe it was just the reality that we have lost the habit of common prayer. And after two years, I stopped advertising it, and my own practice became more haphazard.

I suspect my experience is true of many clergy. At seminary, we are surrounded by a community of prayer, and the practice becomes habitual, even unthinking. If we're lucky, that continues if we are appointed to an assistant position in a large church, where again we are part of a community of leadership and prayer, albeit somewhat less intense. But there is always at least one other person to pray with.

But then we hit solo ministry, and for the vast majority of us there are no social or communal supports for our prayer. Our best intentions crumble, and our lives become haphazard. For many of us, prayer becomes something we do on Sundays and in emergencies.

It seems obvious to say that our preaching should be grounded in and surrounded by prayer. Anything less would seem foolhardy when we are engaged in speaking the word(s) of God. Yet for many of us in parish ministry, the prayer of preaching is all too often confined to a short paragraph at some stage in the preparation processes—most often when we are desperate—the liturgical prayer that surrounds our preached words, and a final brief prayer, "Thank God it's over."

One of the dangers of the preaching life is that we become too busy to stop and take time to speak with God—which is a strange thing for those whose vocation is at its heart about nurturing a relationship between our people and our God. It is easier to do those things that are—or at least seem to be—productive. There is something satisfying about holding in our hands five pages of notes on a biblical text or, even better, a full manuscript for a sermon. But we have nothing to show for an hour with God, nothing tangible at least, which is why many of us, I suspect, do better at the identifiable tasks of ministry—leading worship, preaching, administration, visiting—than the more ephemeral things that underpin it. It's much easier to be accountable for these tasks, to check off the number of services offered, visits made, sermons preached, than the number of hours spent in prayer.

But spending time with God is essential for our life as preachers. If we don't know God, then how can we speak of and for God? What distinguishes preaching from other forms of address is, fundamentally, its character as speech that is simultaneously divine and human. There are other rhetorical forms that seek to change, to transform; other forms seek to make connections between one world and another. In other words, other forms may have the same overall content and purpose; however, preaching alone is *sacred* rhetoric—God is involved, not in the generalized way that God is present and active in all of creation or more particularly in the way that the Holy Spirit is in the lives of Christians, but in a unique and particular way. In the sermon, God's voice is heard—albeit sometimes faintly obscured—but at the heart of a sacramental understanding we assert that God is present in this preaching event, that we can be assured, by grace, of meeting God here.

That makes preaching a fearsome and holy task. And it would be foolhardy to engage in such a task without adequate preparation, without immersion in the One who makes it possible. That immersion we call prayer.

PRAYER IN SCRIPTURE AND TRADITION

Sometimes I wish that the Bible were structured more like a textbook. Instead of having a collection of stories and letters identified by the names of the heroes of our faith, we would have a larger instruction manual with sections labeled by content: ethics, evangelism, prayer, sexuality, money, stewardship, politics, and, of course, preaching.

Even though preaching plays an essential part in the spread of the gospel in early Christianity as described in the New Testament, there is nothing in Scripture about how to go about it. And while we must assume that it has an inherent link with prayer—because we speak about and on behalf of God, and to do that with authenticity requires that we have some sort of personal relationship with God—that preaching and prayer are linked in the lives of our scriptural icons is something that we can only suppose from the sketchy details given us.

It begins with Moses, I suppose, the first one entrusted with the task of delivering words from God to the people. On the Exodus journey, Moses would pitch his tent away from the rest of the camp. God would come to meet with him, speaking face to face as to a friend. And when he and God had met, Moses would gather the people and tell them what God had said. It's as close as we get in the Old Testament to a link between prayer and preaching.

In the New Testament, the connections are both more visible and more removed. Prayer tends to be described more abstractly—no longer do specially chosen individuals meet God face to face, as Moses did, and return with faces glowing to pass on the message. The first disciples came somewhere close, as they traveled with Jesus, Word made flesh, but the next generation had a much less tangible experience of prayer. It's true that instead of waiting for a prophet to be our intermediary with God, they had direct access to God in and through Jesus Christ by the power of the Holy Spirit, but that access didn't typically include an audible or visible response. We have direct access to God in prayer, but sometimes it feels like a figment of our religious imaginations.

But prayer is the essential background for ministry; it's the primary expression of our connectedness to God. Christ prepared for his public ministry with a period in the desert, where we presume he prayed; time and time again he withdrew from the crowds to pray before returning to satisfy their demands in teaching and healing. Paul himself provides an example of prayerful ministry. In the epistles, leaders of the church are urged to make prayer an integral part of their lives. And so the life of prayer is the context of ministry and the foundation for preaching.

And prayer has been foundational for many of the great preachers in history. Lancelot Andrewes, the great seventeenth-century bishop, preacher, and translator of the King James Version of the Bible, is said to have spent five hours per day in prayer; 150 years later, John Wesley prayed for a minimum of two hours. That time spent in prayer gave them an intimacy with God that shines through their preaching.

I don't know how they did it. The pace of the seventeenth and eighteenth centuries was surely less frenetic than that of the twenty-first century; the expectations of clergy were different. But maybe that's just an excuse. Intimacy with God is the foundation of our life as preachers.

Prayer comes in many forms. Most of us grew up with the short, specific prayer that asks—or thanks—God for something. Most often heard before bed, it goes something like this. "Dear God, thank you for Mommy, Daddy, my baby sister, Joey, Ed, Katie, Grandma, Aunt Grace, Scruffy, Bobo, and my worm. Please make Grandpa better. Amen." There might have be a short prayer before meals, "Bless this food to our use, Lord, and us to thy service, and make us ever mindful of the needs of others." Or the one I learned as a five-year-old, said all in one rush of breath, "For-good-food-and-kind-friends-thank-you-God-Amen." And then there are the prayers of panic and helplessness: "Please God, *do* something!"

As preachers, we do a lot of this sort of praying, especially when we have no idea of what we are going to say: "Dear God, please give me *some* idea of what to say about this reading." Or the prayer we pray before we begin the sermon-writing process, a prayer that begins, "Be with me God as I begin this task. Give me wisdom, insight, and clarity, and may your Holy Spirit rest upon me." We might pray a prayer for illumination before entering the pulpit, or begin our sermon with the traditional psalm prayer, "May the words of my lips and the meditations of all our hearts be now and always acceptable to you, O Lord, our strength and our redeemer."

All that is well and good. But our sermons must be undergirded by prayer, and that takes more than a few focused words: As preachers, our lives must be constantly open to God. And that means prayer in all its forms: conversational, habitual, reflective, recreational, liturgical—life imbued and saturated with prayer—and with God.

A CONVERSATION WITH GOD

The most natural form of prayer is conversational. That's where most of us begin as small children, as we share with God the most important people and things in our lives. It's also where many of us end, as increasing physical frailty constricts our worlds and the ministries in which we have served for a lifetime, but leaves us still able to speak, albeit perhaps haltingly, with our Lord. Between visits to families and to the nursing home, I often overhear prayers about the new puppy or the ward guinea pig: Both my youngest parishioners and the elderly residents with dementia assume—rightly, I believe—that God is interested in everything that interests them. And the rest of us are no different. As I travel through the day, my thoughts are peppered with small prayers about the people and places and events of the moment.

In conversational prayer, we talk with God. Sometimes speaking, sometimes falling silent to listen, we share our lives, the everyday dramas and sorrows and rejoicing. I often imagine God and me sitting in big squashy armchairs in a cozy living room, fire burning bright in the hearth, rich red of an Oriental carpet on the floor, books lining the walls. There we sit, sipping coffee or a good single malt, and chat about the day.

We talk to God; we believe that God listens. God talks to us; (hopefully) we listen. Talking to God is relatively straightforward, even if we do it less often than we might; listening is somewhat more difficult, as God does not typically use words audible to the human ear. Prayer is a conversation, an expression of the relationship we have with the Holy One. It is that relationship that underpins our ministry and especially our preaching.

Preaching is itself a conversation with God. If preaching is both human and divine speech by the epicletic grace of the Holy Spirit, we have, in a sense, a conversation with God happening in the preaching moment—a speaking and listening all at the same time. Because we who preach know that what we say is as much a tentative exploration as anything, that we might as well end every sermon, our bold statement of what is and might be, with the childish question, "Isn't it?" I suspect that's why many of us end with that firm declarative "Amen." Because we want to be certain, we hope so desperately with all our hearts and minds and souls and strength that everything we have said is true, but we're always conscious of that doubt that lurks deep in all of our minds: "What if I got it wrong?" The firm declarative "Amen" dispels our doubts, at least for the time being, that what we are saying is mere words plucked from the air, instead affirming our sermon as epicletic speech that is, but by the grace of God, true enough.

But the conversation is not confined to the sermon itself; the sermon is, rather, a coalescence of the conversation which precedes and succeeds it. It is a conversation that reaches back to the time we first began to think about the sermon, first uttered a breath of prayer to God, "Help me," first opened the Scriptures, and reaches also beyond that to the larger conversation which began when we first became conscious of God, and beyond that to our conception, and beyond that to the conversation of faith that reaches back to creation itself. It is a conversation that also reaches forward, looking toward the consummation of all things.

And it's a conversation that continues beyond the moment we step down from the pulpit. It continues liturgically, in the Eucharist, when we experience the presence of Christ; it continues practically as the words of the sermon resonate in our lives and become part of the ordinary to-and-fro between us and God; it continues eschatologically until the consummation of all things.

That's why it's dangerous to think of prayer in relation to preaching as simply that intuitive act we engage in when we're blocked on writing, or the sometimes confident, sometimes panicked prayer we shoot up as we enter the pulpit. Prayer soaks our lives; it waters the ground and allows the plant of our vocation to grow and bear fruit.

Our lives need to be steeped in prayer, in that continual conversation between God and us that develops in this strange thing when the voice of God and our voices muddle together and we speak, by the grace of the Holy Spirit, such that people may hear God.

Conversational prayer is, however, largely haphazard. It's prayer that happens when we walk into the room and pause to chat with someone there, when we have something that we need help with and make a phone call, when we have something to share and invite a friend over. To have lives steeped in prayer, we need to be a little more deliberate. That is the place of habitual prayer. This is the habit of prayer that day in, day out, sustains our faith, the prayer that we do whether we believe or not.

HABITS OF FAITH

When I was a child, on the bookcase at the head of my bed, alongside the ever-changing array of library books, were a Bible and a small paperback book. In that book were readings for each day for three months at a time, along with questions to answer, puzzles to do, and suggestions for prayer. It was part of my religious tradition and upbringing to have a daily "quiet time," time consciously spent on the company of God to read, reflect, and pray. When I missed it, my day felt somehow incomplete. It is a habit that built a firm foundation for the faith that has sustained me these last forty years.

This habitual prayer did not, however, begin with the advent of individual Bibles and prayer aids. Long before the advent of the printing press, people gathered morning and evening—and oftentimes in between—to pray. It happened in monasteries, in cathedrals and parish churches, and in private chapels in homes. We have inherited this practice in the form of the daily office, short liturgical services focused around the reading of Scripture and response in prayer. Morning, noonday, evening, and night, these prayers create a rhythm to the day that instills an awareness of God. And for those of us who find chatting with an invisible God difficult, they invite us into structured conversation. The words line up on the page, and we follow the route mapped out before us, sinking into the prayers and psalms that speak on our behalf. And whether we pray the offices alone or congregationally, we are part of a community of prayer that reaches back hundreds of years and across thousands of miles.

We thank thee that thy Church, unsleeping
while earth rolls onward into light,
through all the world her watch is keeping
and rests not now by day nor night.

As o'er each continent and island
the dawn leads on another day,
the voice of prayer is never silent,
nor dies the strain of praise away.

The sun that bids us rest is waking
our brethren 'neath the western sky,
and hour by hour fresh lips are making
thy wondrous doings heard on high.

—John Ellerton, 1870

Last year I spent a few days on the Holy Island of Lindisfarne in northern England. It is a place deeply saturated with prayer, a millennium and a half deep, reaching back to Cuthbert and Aidan and Cedd. Every morning and every evening, people gather to pray in the small church of St. Mary the Virgin, morning prayer and evening prayer, joining their prayers with those of fifteen centuries of worship. As a visitor, I was swept up into that rhythm of prayer, morning and evening, an active attentiveness to God that continues whether or not we are paying attention.

Habitual prayer feeds our preaching in an unexpected way. The language of prayer soaks itself into our minds and hearts, and we find phrases from our prayers seep into the very words that we preach. They enrich our vocabulary; more importantly, they evoke a sense of familiarity for our hearers who have prayed the same prayers, they echo the scriptural sources of the office. The words of our sermons settle themselves into our hearers' memories; they become part of a wider fabric of God-talk that feeds and expresses our faith.

SITTING QUIETLY WITH GOD

But not all prayer is active. Some of it, to use my earlier image, is simply about sitting in the same room as God, sharing each other's presence. The practice of reflective prayer—whether it takes the form of meditation, contemplative prayer, or *lectio divina*—is a time-honored expression of our relationship with God. The quiet stillness allows our hearts and souls to rest in the presence of the beloved. And just as those newly in love glow with the joy of their relationship, we can't help but preach with passion when we have spent that sort of time with God, when our hearts and souls have been caught up into the holiness of God.

> The mind that comes to rest is tended
> In ways that it cannot intend:
> Is borne, preserved, and comprehended
> By what it cannot comprehend.
>
> Your Sabbath, Lord, thus keeps us by
> Your will, not ours. And it is fit
> Our only choice should be to die
> Into that rest, or out of it.

"Sabbath," Wendell Berry (born 1934)

I have to admit that I am not a contemplative by nature. I have good memories of times spent on a prayer stool in a rough mud-brick chapel, but for the most part, I get impatient after about ten minutes of sitting quietly waiting for God. Stilling our bodies may be an aid to prayer; it also may be a barrier. Quiet repetitious movement may help us to pray reflectively. Some people find walking a labyrinth or knitting a prayer shawl frees their minds, hearts, and souls to wait on God. I find myself more open to God as I hike through the hills of Northumbria or along the beach at the Jersey Shore or beside the Housatonic River in northwest Connecticut. Perhaps what that reflects is that like many Christians, my relationship with God echoes that with my father—and what I enjoy most with him is spending time doing things together—at an art gallery or in the car or walking the streets of London, content just to be with one another, not needing to fill the space with unnecessary chatter. Our presence with one another and the love that reflects is at the core of our relationship.

When we pray reflectively, we open ourselves to God. The absence of an agenda invites God to work in our unconscious mind, bringing to the surface ideas and emotions of which we are not consciously aware. Often it is when we engage with God in this way that we are at our most creative. In preparing our sermons, it is here that the Spirit works, making unexpected connections, redirecting our focus, giving us language to speak the holy words of God. And when we read Scripture in the context of reflective prayer, as suggested in chapter 3, we find unexpected insights and emphases, guided by the Holy Spirit.

RE-CREATION

Closely related to reflective prayer is what I like to call "recreational prayer," the prayer that re-creates and renews us. This is Sabbath prayer: Praying and playing are the two sides of the Sabbath. We play in the presence of God, and our awareness of that presence is expressed in prayer. We are like children absorbed in a game, and yet at the same time conscious enough of our mother sitting over on the park bench to throw an occasional glance and say, "Did you see me, Mommy? Did you see me?" Of course, we are always under that tender gaze; Sabbath is the time when we are free to appreciate it, and perhaps unencumbered enough to run over occasionally for no apparent reason and throw our arms around that loving watcher. Sabbath allows us space to play, and space to pray, a space of grace.

〰

William, Matilda, and Emma-Li,
Lucy, Sophia, and Johnny

Owen, Catharine, and Talia too
Anna Maria and Hani

Together they played throughout the day
jumping and leaping and swinging

Together they prayed throughout the day
dancing and swirling and singing

Anne E. Kitch, *Bless This Way* (Harrisburg, PA:
Morehouse Publishing, 2003). Used by permission.

And that is the heart of it. Grace. Too often Sabbath has become another occasion for works—a time when we have to "be good" because God is watching. The nineteenth-century strictures about what one could or couldn't do—no reading of novels or anything else frivolous, no games, the day to be spent studying Scripture, praying, and writing letters—missed the point. This is about grace! And grace is a playful, passionate thing.

But grace is also, at its heart, relational. Grace is about being in a relationship with our Savior, a relationship that is life-giving rather than life-denying. And just as it is effectively impossible to have any sort of relationship without communication, it is impossible for us to have a relationship with God without communication—and the primary way we communicate is prayer.

But the prayer of Sabbath is not so much an earnest, wordy thing, as it is that activity of playing in God's presence. It's like seeing a good friend after a long absence, or perhaps sitting down with a lover after a day at work and enjoying a glass of wine together. Few words may be spoken, but there is the look, the touch, the exchange of breath. That companionability, that expressed love, is the prayer of Sabbath.

Of course, it looks somewhat different, because we can't actually see God sitting in the comfortable old armchair with the dented cushions. And so we cultivate a Sabbath awareness, a state in which we constantly turn to God with thankful observation, like a child showing a new discovery. "Look God! See that tulip. Its petals are raggy and soft, almost like a rose. Touch this, God! Doesn't my cat's belly fur feel like velvet? Hey God, did you know. . . ?" That's the prayer of Sabbath.

The prayer of Sabbath feeds our preaching. In full awareness of the presence of God, we suddenly see God's hand at work—in everything. And that is the heart of what we need to speak in preaching—God at work in our world.

MORE THAN WORDS

Our preaching is steeped in prayer, not only in the preparation phases, but perhaps more importantly in its delivery. We preach in the context of common prayer.

∼◡

Prayers from Tradition

Before beginning preparation:

Blessed Lord, who hast caused all holy Scriptures to be written for our learning;
Grant that we may in such wise hear them read, mark, learn, and inwardly digest them,
that by patience, and comfort of thy holy Word,
we may embrace, and ever hold fast the blessed hope of everlasting life,
which thou hast given us in our Saviour Jesus Christ. Amen.

Book of Common Prayer (1662), Collect for the second Sunday in Advent

For the congregation:

Stir up, we beseech thee, O Lord, the wills of thy faithful people;
that they, plenteously bringing forth the fruit of good works,
may of thee be plenteously rewarded;
through Jesus Christ our Lord. Amen.

Book of Common Prayer (1662),
Collect for the twenty-fifth Sunday after Trinity

For us as we prepare:
Come, Holy Ghost, our souls inspire,
and lighten with celestial fire.
Thou the anointing Spirit art,
who dost thy sevenfold gifts impart.

Thy blessed unction from above
is comfort, life, and fire of love.
Enable with perpetual light
the dullness of our blinded sight.

Anoint and cheer our soiled face
with the abundance of thy grace.
Keep far from foes, give peace at home:
where thou art guide, no ill can come.

Teach us to know the Father, Son,
and thee, of both, to be but One,
that through the ages all along,
this may be our endless song:

Praise to thy eternal merit,
Father, Son, and Holy Spirit.

Veni Creator Spiritus, ninth century; trans. John Cosin, 1627

For us and our congregation as we preach:

Almighty God, unto whom all hearts be open, all desires known, and whom
no secrets are hid; Cleanse the thoughts of our hearts by the inspiration of thy
Holy Spirit, that we may perfectly love thee and worthily magnify thy holy
Name; through Christ our Lord, Amen.

Book of Common Prayer (1662)

Corporate prayer is the background to all our preaching, and for
those of us in liturgical traditions, that corporate prayer takes a liturgical
form. Our forebears read and prayed, and crafted words that became the
skeleton of the prayers that structure our worship today. Their prayers
echo Scripture, phrases woven in so that God's word becomes our words,
which we then speak back to God. They give voice to the things we want
to say but struggle to articulate. Even when we use new words of prayer,
from recent liturgical texts or from our own hearts and souls, the same
thing exists—a patchwork of words drawn from Scripture, older prayers,
and our own lives that give voice to the human longing for God. But they
are more than words. The words are the framework in which the Spirit
dwells. This is God's work—God's grace—that makes a somewhat haphazard collection of words into holy conversation.

We don't have to say everything. The liturgy does that for us. And
into it we drop the sermon, our halting words for and about God, which,
at their best, soar above with promise and risk over this safety net of prayer.

Love Came to Us
A Sermon

Sometimes Scripture catches us unawares. It was like that for me yesterday, as I began preparing this sermon. It can be hard to muster up any enthusiasm for church again, so soon after the busyness of Christmas. I'd figured I'd preach on something I'd preached on before, the reading from the Gospel of John, chapter 1, those well-known words, "In the beginning was the Word, and the Word was with God and the Word was God. He was in the beginning with God."

But just to stop myself from feeling too guilty, I'd read through the other readings before I began, just to set it all into context. And it was then, when I opened up my Bible at Isaiah chapter 61, that I was captivated by the words of our first reading.

"I will greatly rejoice in the LORD, my whole being shall exult in my God; for he has clothed me with the garments of salvation, he has covered me with the robe of righteousness, as a bridegroom decks himself with a garland, and as a bride adorns herself with her jewels."

There is an incredible sense here that the person speaking here is loved by God, is regarded as precious, and they know it.

It reminds me of a newborn baby, being held in the arms of her mother or father, and being totally secure, totally safe, totally loved. There is nothing outside that incredible circle of love.

In the reading from Isaiah, though, it is not a baby that is receiving this love, but an adult, the servant of the Lord. This is the one of whom it was written, in the opening verses of Isaiah chapter 61: "The spirit of the Lord GOD is upon me, because the LORD has anointed me; he has sent me to bring good news to the oppressed, to bind up the brokenhearted, to proclaim liberty to the captives, and release to the prisoners; to proclaim the year of the Lord's favor, and the day of vengeance of our God."

They are words that are familiar to us, from early on in the Gospel of Luke, words that Jesus read when he went to the synagogue in Nazareth and read from the book of Isaiah — and finished with the words, "Today this Scripture has been fulfilled in your hearing." This person that is so dearly loved by God is, from our perspective as Christians, this person is Jesus Christ, that little baby, born in Bethlehem, God made flesh.

But as I read those words from Isaiah, I was reminded of other words: For you are "a chosen race, a royal priesthood, a holy nation, God's own people, in order that you may proclaim the mighty acts of him who called you out of darkness into his marvelous light." They are words from the first letter of Peter, in the New Testament. And, in other places in the New Testament, the church is described as the bride of Christ.

All that suggests that, like Christ, God has clothed us with the garments of salvation, covered us with the robe of righteousness, as a bridegroom decks himself with a garland, and as a bride adorns herself with her jewels.

Imagine the most gorgeous designer clothing, the most stunning jewelry. It is as if God has gone out and chosen those for us, and wrapped us in them, silks and velvet and brocades, diamonds and rubies and emeralds. All to show just how much we are loved.

Sometimes it seems hardly possible that we could be loved like this. Something happens between babyhood and adulthood, somewhere in those early years of childhood. We suddenly realize that the whole world doesn't in fact revolve around us, that we are not really the focus of everyone's love. We begin, most of us, knowing ourselves to be loved and lovable, beautiful, precious, simply because we are here. And we love everyone in return, we see beauty all around us, we hold everyone and everything dear. And then, over time, we discover that maybe love isn't the only force in the world. Maybe we aren't beautiful in everyone's eyes. We are disillusioned, stripped of the illusion of love. That circle of love and beauty, which once encompassed everything we knew, becomes smaller and smaller until many of us can't even remember what it was like. That's part of what it is to grow up. Life is tough. People say things that hurt us. They betray us. We learn that we aren't perfect, nor is anyone else. It becomes safer to ration out our love. And many of us, deep down inside, begin to come to the conclusion that we are not really worthy of love.

Sometimes we catch glimpses of that original vision, that sense of beauty and love, perhaps with a partner or a child, but always we have in the background the fear that, just like when we grew up, one day it will be gone, and we'll be back to the stark reality of our unlovableness.

Except. Except the truth of it all is that we are not unlovable. The truth of it all is that we are loved, loved dearly by one who wants to wrap us in silk and satin and velvet, to shower us with diamonds and rubies and emeralds. We are loved by God from the tops of our heads to the soles of our feet, from the times when we are most confident to the deepest, darkest places within us, we are loved.

We are the precious children of God, loved from the time we are conceived to the time we die, when we are happy and when we are sad we are loved, when we are sick and when we are healthy we are loved, when we are faithful and when we are faithless we are loved.

It is one of those truths that is almost too good to be believed, but it is true all the same. We are loved.

And how do we know it? Because of Jesus, that most-loved Son of God. Because God so loved the world that he gave his only Son. In the midst of darkness, God sent light. In the midst of death, God sent life. In the midst of disillusion, God sent love.

The Gospel of John is full of it. In the beginning was the Word and that Word became flesh and lived among us in the person of Jesus Christ. Jesus himself embodied the love of God; he was, as John reminds us, the only Son of God and, as the book of Hebrews reminds us, the very image and likeness of God. In Jesus, we can know God. In Jesus we can know the love of God which pours out on us in all its fullness. Because in him the fullness of God was pleased to dwell, the fullness of God that has, at its heart, love, and that fullness of God came among us in Jesus Christ. Love came to us, love incarnate, love divine, and we are truly loved. Even when we feel most unlovable, we are loved, wrapped in the precious garments of salvation and righteousness—not because of who we are, but because of who God is, the great creator and lover of all.

Sunday, December 28, 2003—Christmas 1, Year C
Isaiah 61:10–62:3; John 1:1–18
Trinity Episcopal "Old Swedes" Church, Swedesboro, New Jersey

Take, Eat
A Sermon

I can still remember the feel of summer vacations when I was a kid.

There were those first delicious days of anticipation where it seemed that anything was possible, the first trip to the beach, a sleep-over, and the promise of a visit with my grandparents. Time seemed endless, and life was wonderful.

But as the weeks wore on, the signs of the end increasingly encroached on my summer. There was the inevitable trip to the mall for new shoes—not much time left for bare feet—pencils to be labeled, and three months' worth of piano practice to be done.

Summer is just three months of the year, but in those three months we have a microcosm of our lives at large.

As children, our lives stretch before us. We play at being firefighters and soldiers and teachers, we imagine ourselves as ballerinas and astronauts, and our lives are full of possibility and adventure.

But as we grow older, it's all too clear that the end of the summer is not so far away. Our dreams lose their glistening feathers and fall to the ground and get trampled under our own feet. We must be sensible and prudent and prepare for our retirement. Our bodies begin to creak and groan—the first gray hairs, the aches which might just be the beginnings of arthritis, and a simple tiredness that seems to come from nowhere. And the world around us and the ideal life presented on TV become further and further from the secure reality we once knew.

The end of the summer: Our bodies betray us, our choices condemn us, our world bears down on us. Death and life become muddled together.

And then we hear Jesus, and he seems to be just as caught up in the muddle as we are.

"I am the bread of life, the bread come down from heaven," he says. "Whoever eats of this bread will never die; whoever believes has eternal life."

And the people around him stare, and some laugh, because they know his father and his mother, know that this is no heavenly apparition but just young Jesus bar Joseph, son of a carpenter, vagabond and storyteller. And for all that he made a feast for five thousand from a few loaves and fishes, they will all be hungry again, and he will be too, and they will all die, whether from famine or illness, in a skirmish with the occupying troops, or, if God is gracious, as righteous elders at home in their beds.

We all know that death will eventually come. We can prolong our lives with healthy lifestyles and good medical care, we can fight against the diseases and the violence that ravish our world, but in the end we will all die, and there's no way of avoiding it.

And these claims of Jesus of eternal life are as muddled as anything else. Because, on the one hand, there is a security about it, the idea that death isn't the end of everything, that the people we love are safely waiting somewhere, looking forward to a joyous reunion, but, on the other, there is always the fear that comes from the skepticism of our world that we're just kidding ourselves. That this heaven thing is about as unreal as those little round-eyed children on the Precious Moments cards, and we'd better get on with life in the grainy reality of the here and now.

We can just about deal with Easter and the resurrection, as long as it's only Jesus, but when it comes to us, it's a whole 'nother story. Because heaven, and life eternal with it, has got a bad name.

We're embarrassed, most of us, by those people who walk the streets demanding of strangers, "Have you been washed in the blood of the lamb?" Who knock on our doors asking, "If you were to die tonight, what would you say at the gates of heaven?"

It smacks of the pious righteousness we all too often associate with a joyless fanatical religion, one in which we are expected to leave our brains outside the church doors.

And so, it seems to me, in response, sometimes we go to the other extreme. We avoid talking about heaven or anything which could possibly be construed as otherworldly, and we focus our attention on the world around us. Instead of focusing on some ethereal kingdom of God after death, we focus on bringing about that kingdom of God in the here and now. We might not use those words for it, but that's what we're doing as we seek transformation in our own lives, and as we work to bring that transformation into other people's lives as well. And so we get active in the local community, with Motel Meals and Crisis Ministry, the Trenton After School Program and Done in a Day. And that's certainly part of the Christian gospel. But it's not the whole of it. Because there's no getting around it—what Jesus is talking about in today's Gospel is about life and death, and life after death.

Part of the problem is that there are no real details about what this life after death will be like. We get glimpses throughout the New Testament—transformed bodies, no more tears, some sort of closeness to God, but nothing really tangible, nothing we can grasp hold of with the kind of certainty we'd like, certainly nothing that could be considered as proof. Of course, there's Jesus's resurrection, but even that doesn't tell us a whole lot more.

But I want to say that today's reading fills in just a little bit of that picture, and it does it in a way that maybe, just maybe, begins to make a connection between the kingdom of God in heaven and the kingdom of God here on earth, between eternal life after death and eternal life which is now.

Jesus talks of himself as the bread of life. Eating this bread, whatever that means, somehow brings eternal life—and, of course, bread is on his hearers' minds. The way John tells the story, Jesus speaks these words the day after he had fed the five thousand; those same people are here to hear him again, full of the bread they ate by the lakeside. This bread is as real and satisfying as the crumbs that lie heavily on their stomachs. And this bread is as real and as satisfying as the manna was in the desert, which, if you remember the story in Exodus, saved the Israelites from starvation as they wandered in the wilderness. Bread is a staple: Time and time again in the Old Testament God uses bread to save the people.

This bread is the bread from heaven, bread which brings life now and forever. And all they have to do is eat it; all they have to do is believe.

It's both like and unlike our friends who ask what we would say at the gate of heaven.

Heaven, yes, whatever or wherever that might be, but certainly eternal life, but you don't have to get the right answer. Getting eternal life isn't about passing an exam, or even proving your worthiness. It's about being offered a plate of bread, taking a piece, and eating it. Even a child knows how to do that. And God will turn no one away who knows how to eat.

Which means us—and the whole world. For this bread Jesus gave for the life of the world, the bread of his flesh.

Here and now, in this world as in the next, God reaches out with bread to feed our souls, to bring us wholeness, to heal the world. So that we in turn may reach out, to bring to the world that same feeding and wholeness and healing.

And so we, here each Sunday, hang on for dear life to these peculiar rituals, reaching out empty hands for a piece of bread and the very life of God.

Take, eat, this is my body broken for you. Do this in remembrance of me.

August 13, 2000—Proper 14, Year B
Deuteronomy 8:1–10; John 6:35–51
Trinity Episcopal Church, Princeton, New Jersey

· 7 ·

And It Was Very Good: Embodiment

$\mathcal{O}$ne of the great delights of parish ministry is watching the children at our early service. Nathan, aged two, kneels with his head barely showing over the altar rail and hands raised high to receive the bread and wine; afterward, he stays at the rail for the rest of the service, entranced by the pageantry and by being up close to it all. Rachel, just starting school, walks solemnly up to fetch the small Salvadoran cross to lead the gospel procession, holding it as high as she can with her nose pressed against the pole to keep it straight, then absentmindedly skips back to her parents' pew; Robert and James's voices sound high above the adults in the Lord's Prayer, half a beat behind as they struggle to read the words; and the bright orange cast on Luke's arm barely gets in the way as he processes the gospel book into the midst of the congregation. Tyler grins as he carefully carries the collection plate to the altar during the offertory, and bows deeply toward the altar (or sometimes to the congregation) when he is done; Chloe and Kaitlyn have just discovered their voices and squeal and babble along with the sermon; Adam offers a huge toothless smile to his big brother and to me as I bless him; and a chorus of high-pitched voices shout our liturgy's final "Alleluia! Alleluia!"

I need Nathan and Rachel, Robert and James, Luke and Tyler, Chloe and Kaitlyn and Adam—and Jacob, Megan, Alyssa, Sophia, Cody, Zach, Hunter, Justin, Christopher, Lauren, Patrick, Logan, Aidan, Emma, and all the other kids at church—to remind me that worship, this somewhat peculiar thing we do on Sunday mornings, is not just an exercise of the mind and the imagination. Worship for them involves all their senses; it is a visceral, physical experience that requires

131

their participation in every part of their beings. All their senses are engaged; they worship God with the whole of their bodies.

Children's songs are a perfect example. We're quite happy to sing "If I Were a Butterfly" with elaborate actions when we are young, but as we grow older, our gestures become smaller and smaller, and by the time we are adults we'd rather die than embarrass ourselves by behaving like an elephant. When we're small, we sing and dance a Christian equivalent to the hokey pokey:

> God's not dead, he is alive!
> God's not dead, he is alive!
> God's not dead, he is alive!
>
> I can feel him in my hands,
> I feel him in my feet,
> I hear him in the church,
> And I hear him in the street. . . .

But as adults, even the invitation to clap along leaves many of us feeling awkward and unsure.

Somehow, somewhere in the process of growing up, most of us lose that intensely physical engagement in worship that is so evident in children. Faith moves from our bodies to our heads, and we forget the joy of our createdness. We may retain a vestige of it in our liturgy—in the Episcopal tradition, the actions of standing, sitting, and kneeling echo in our bodies what is happening in our minds and hearts; other traditions may raise their hands high or clap—but often we sit in pews as if church were a college lecture. Our bodies become marginalized from our faith, and our relationship with the One who looked upon the first human beings on day six of creation and saw that it was very good is impoverished.

> Praise the God who made our bodies,
> nerve and muscle, flesh and blood,
> made us in God's own true image,
> male and female, holy good.
> Glorify the God who made us!
> Use our bodies to explore

all the world, with all our senses,
daily learning more and more.

Praise the God who, born of Mary,
made salvation's pattern plain,
grew among us, knew our limits,
hungered, wept, and died in pain.
Glorify the God who saves us,
came to heal us, gave us grace!
In our bodies, gladly worship
God, who has a human face.

Praise the God whose church is living
as a body, Spirit-filled,
God, whose wisdom longs to make us
one in love, as Jesus willed.
Glorify the God who called us!
Use our bodies to proclaim
all the Holy Spirit's message,
all the power of Jesus' name.

—Elizabeth J. Smith
Suggested music: Abbot's Leigh
Used by permission

We are incarnate beings. Our bodies are our selves. Faith inherently concerns us. And so our faith is intimately involved with our bodies.

As preachers, the connection between our faith and our bodies is even more pronounced. We use our voices when we preach, but we also use the rest of our bodies—gestures with our hands, expressiveness in our faces, movement in our legs and feet. Some preachers walk up and down the aisle or across the sanctuary, others of us might stay in the pulpit, but few of us stand rigidly at attention as we speak. Anyone who has injured a leg and had to preach with crutches or from a stool or chair knows how essential our bodies are. With only restricted use, it is as if our preaching voices are muffled. Our bodies matter for us as preachers.

CLAD IN THE GOODNESS OF GOD

One of the great omissions in Scripture is any clear teaching on the logistics of preaching—descriptions of sermons in the book of Acts, for example, provide the content of those first sermons, but little about what it looked like to see the early disciples preach—or any explicit theology of the role of the literal physical body in ministry. When thinking homiletically, we have to extract more general teaching on the body and then apply it to our preaching context.

It all begins in the first chapter of Genesis. God creates human beings, male and female, and they are part of the good creation. But it doesn't take long for ambiguity to creep in. The snake persuades Eve to take a piece of fruit, she gives it to Adam, he eats it, and creation begins to unravel. And the first casualty is the body—Adam and Eve cover themselves, because they are ashamed. In the space of a few verses, the body has gone from being part of the glory of creation to a source of shame.

This ambiguity about bodies continues in Scripture. On the one hand, Levitical precepts protect people's bodies from abuse; on the other, certain essential parts of the body—such as blood—are deemed capable of rendering people unclean for worship. The Song of Songs celebrates human love in its bodily expression; in other writings, denying one's bodily needs and desires, whether nutritional or sexual, is a sign of faithfulness.

In the New Testament, the ambiguity persists. In the letters to the Corinthians, the body is both the temple of the Holy Spirit and an obstacle to union with Christ; physical needs are to be met, but desires often to be curbed for the sake of the gospel. While moderation appears to be the ideal set forth, the many restrictions placed on the body, especially when heard through the filter of our philosophical inheritance of a body/soul split, give the impression that bodies are a necessary evil. No wonder we are confused!

But there is one exception, and it is the exception at the heart of our faith: Jesus Christ himself. For if nothing else, the very act of the incarnation tips the scales decisively in favor of the body. What was merely speech in the first book of Genesis—that all creation, including human beings, is good—becomes an event: God made flesh, come among us. There can be no inherent contradiction between the goodness of God and the status of the body. If God took human form, then human form—our existence as embodied beings—must be inherently good. That's the gift of the incarnation.

The incarnation is a great theological concept, but I sometimes wonder if we don't tend to forget the reality of it. At Christmas, we coo over a baby in a manger; the incarnation means that Mary went through who knows how many hours of body-wrenching labor; diapers and spit-up and angry wails of hunger were an indispensable part of Jesus's early life. Later on, he not only affirmed the necessity of embodied experience when he provided food for the hungry thousands and restored to whole-ness those who were blind and crippled and ill, but was himself subject to the embodied experience of being human: He got hungry and thirsty and footsore on the road, and he feasted with friends; he got tired and sneaked away to rest; he used his hands and even saliva as vehicles of God's grace. And in the final act of life, his body was subjected to tor-ture and pain, scoured, speared, nailed to a cross.

It was then, and only then, that his body was transformed. Having lived an embodied existence, his physical body became the sign of a new existence, that of resurrected life. In spite of our tendency to make a split between body and soul or spirit, it was as a body that Christ rose, some-how transformed, yet still bearing the scars of spear and thorns and nails.

And, of course, the final vindication for the body comes in the Eu-charist, when Christ's body and our bodies mingle, and we ourselves, the church, are the body of Christ.

It's no wonder then, that there has been such a strong reaction over the centuries against movements that seek to separate the soul or spirit from the body. Whether it's from Platonic philosophy, Gnostic heresy, or Cartesian worldviews, time and time again the church has reclaimed the body as holy. Julian of Norwich describes it beautifully: "For as the body is clad in the cloth, and the flesh in the skin, and the bones in the flesh, and the heart in the trunk, so are we, soul and body, clad and en-closed in the goodness of God."[1] We are our bodies, and our bodies em-body our faith.

Preaching is an act of faith, then, that requires the fusion of mind, body, and spirit. Our bodies are an essential part of this act of ministry. And so, just as we attend to the other spiritual disciplines that underpin our preaching, so we must attend to our bodies. Our ability to preach literally depends on it: Voice and movement are vehicles of grace. Our ability to preach depends on our embodied existence, as we speak from the experience of living in the midst of creation.

WORD MADE FLESH

Our bodies are vehicles of grace. God works in and through us to speak to the church, the people of God. We tend, in our culture, to make a split between the physical and the spiritual, but in preaching the physical *is* spiritual. In preaching, we incarnate the Word. Jana Childers expresses it this way: "The gospel, like preaching, is about the Word that gets inside us, that takes up dwelling in us; the Word that speaks and is spoken through human mouths; the Word that impregnates us though the ear."[2] What that means is that our bodies matter.

When it comes to talking about the role of the body in preaching, the place where many people begin is the preacher's appearance. Some advocate particular styles of dress; others give advice on hairstyles. My favorite is the early-mid twentieth-century homiletician, Andrew Blackwood, who advises young clergy:

> Before you go into the sanctuary, think about your personal appearance. Conform with parish custom about wearing a robe or a clerical collar, perhaps both. Put on black shoes, polished with care fore and aft; if shirt and collar appear at all, let each look whiter than snow. Let all your garments come to the sanctuary "unspotted from the world." With face neatly shaved and hair closely trimmed, show everyone that you love the holiness of beauty.[3]

Blackwood's advice for preachers might seem hopelessly anachronistic, and yet behind it lies an important truth. Like it or not, our bodies matter for our preaching. It can be as simple as our congregation intuiting from our appearance what importance we give to this preaching act. If we look sloppy and unkempt, they may decide—rightly or wrongly— that this preaching thing doesn't really matter. On the other hand, if we are beautifully dressed and manicured, they may decide that this is just another processional engagement, something that is more about appearance than deeper reality. We can't control those leaps of inference; what we can be, however, is people of integrity. The way we present ourselves as preachers should be consistent with our message, and that means being aware enough of ourselves to ask whether how we look is congruent with our message, and aware enough of our community to ask whether they will interpret how we look as supporting what we say.

However important our appearance may be, for most if us it is cloaked in vestments: gowns, cassocks, albs, and chasubles. While they may be things of beauty in themselves, they hide all but our most dramatic gestures. If Albert Mehrabian's research is accurate, that after the body, the next most significant aspect of communication is the voice (with the words actually spoken coming a distant third), then our voices are crucially important. [4] With our bodies obscured, our voices achieve much greater prominence and power in Christian proclamation.

～○

God our creator:
You spoke,
and the world came into being.
You spoke,
and came to live among us as Jesus Christ, the Word incarnate.
You spoke,
and with the gift of the Holy Spirit gave life to our speaking.
Thank you for the gift of language
with which we express our thoughts, our hopes, our fears. . . .

～○

Our voices echo God's voice. It was the voice of God that rumbled creation into being, the voice of the Lord that called Israel into faith and back into faith. The voice of the Lord inspired the prophets. The voice of the Lord was incarnate in Jesus, the Word made flesh: "The voice of the Lord is mighty in operation; the voice of the Lord is a powerful voice."[5]

As preachers, our voices stand in for God's voice, with all the power and fearfulness that implies. But when we speak, it is not only God's voice that is heard but ours as well, full of thought, emotion, impulse, and response. And our hearers will, whether we want them to or not, take meaning from our voices.

Likewise, our gestures—even masked by vestments and obscured by distance—are a key part of our communication. When we stand rigidly at attention in the pulpit, white knuckles gripping the railing, we may be saying something about God. When we wander back and forth, turning from one side to another, we may be saying something about God. When we look at people on one side of the church and not the other, we may be saying something about God. We may not intend to say it, but people hear and see it all the same.

It's no wonder that people in need pressed against Jesus and begged him to touch them. When he fed thousands on a grassy hillside, he first looked toward heaven and blessed the food. When Peter sat by the fire that night before his master died, it was not until Jesus looked at him that he realized the magnitude of his betrayal. Jesus's body—his hands, his face, his eyes—gave a message that his words alone could not.

The same is true for us. Our arms, our faces, our voices, all tell the story of what we are trying to say. They are not just packaging; they are part of the message itself.

And that means we need to be aware of how our arms, faces, voices are talking, to be aware of how they work and how they need to be cared for. Sometimes that means paying a little more attention: In my case, I speak quickly and with an Australian accent, so I need to remind my-self—in extra-large print at the top of my sermon manuscript—to slow down, and to make sure that people have had the opportunity to hear my voice and adjust to my accent before getting to the meat of my ser-mon. I also talk with hands in ordinary conservation, and in the pulpit these become large gestures and constant movement. I need to plan and mark the gestures that are most important, and check out the space be-fore I preach so that I don't fall backward off a step!

This sort of attention to practical detail is important: Our preach-ing is more than words. Sometimes it can be helpful to seek out voice lessons or take yoga or find people willing to watch us and tell us when our words and actions aren't quite congruent.[6] These activities can help us to build skills in our bodies to support the spoken word. They help bring the sermon to life.

But the connection is more than practical; it is also spiritual. Body and soul are inextricably entwined.

Most of the time, we don't even notice it. The very fact that we are created in the image of God means that body and soul cooperate; they work as one. But sometimes that unity becomes a problem—because when our bodies break down, our souls are affected too. Preaching is an intensely physical activity, and when our bodies are not functioning properly, it shows—not just in bags under our eyes and croaky voices, but in an underlying malaise of the soul. Caring for our bodies is therefore an essential spiritual practice. Exercise, rest, care in what we eat and drink, attentiveness to our emotions, all matter for our preaching.

As a child, I wasn't a big fan of sports. I came second last in almost every race. I fumbled balls. I was the last person chosen for a team. I retreated into the world of my mind. But two years ago, I was inspired to go on an eighty-four-mile hike across northern England. I joined a gym to prepare my muscles. I drove to state parks to walk on my day off. I got bruises and blisters, but after six months of hard work, I took the first steps along the ruins of Hadrian's Wall. It was a wonderful experience.

But what was most unexpected was how this practice of exercise affected my spiritual life. I found myself acutely aware of the presence of God, the one who made me. I had a sense, for perhaps the first time in my life, that this was who I was created to be, mind and soul and body in complete harmony with each other and with my Creator. And it is from this unity of mind, soul, and body that I preach.

AN OCCASION FOR GRACE

Embodiment, however, is not just about how we use our bodies. More broadly, it is about how we incarnate the gospel, about how we make connections between the world of God and our world. Speaking theologically, this is related to the Chalcedonian definition. As Christ was the nexus, the point of contact between God and humanity, so our preaching should be a point of contact, a somewhat uneasy coalition, between God's world and our world, between the word of God and our words.

If preaching remains abstract, remote from our daily lives, then our hearers are hardly likely to make sense of how it is that they are supposed to *live* as Christians 24/7. And so we strive to connect, to make this God-talk concrete in the language of everyday life. Jesus was good at this: holding up a coin, pointing to a lily, drawing attention to a fishing net. The stuff of ordinary life became an occasion for preaching, an occasion for grace.

The time-honored way of connecting sermon and ordinary life is through the use of the illustration. There are numerous texts that describe this, and a plethora of books and websites full of brief anecdotes designed to be dropped into a sermon at the appropriate moment.

The problem with these is exactly that. Too often they have the feel of something that has been plucked from the air and inserted in the sermon text to provide some light relief, a little sugar to make it palatable.

Even narrative preaching can fall victim to the same trap. There the stories and experiences are at the heart of the sermon, but if we are not careful, they can take over, overpowering God's world so that we are left with just the memory of a story. It's easy to do, to think you have come up with the perfect illustration, one that can be lovingly crafted so that the words bring a picture to the hearers' imaginations. I remember looking out my window one day as I was working on a sermon, and seeing my bird feeder, complete with tufted titmice, chickadees, and of course squirrels lurking underneath, and I thought what a great illustration it would make. I crafted the words carefully, inviting my hearers to my window. And they came—person after person commented on how vividly they could "see" the bird feeder. The only problem was, that was all they remembered about the sermon. I welcomed them into the world of my bird feeder, but failed to welcome them into the world of God.

And that experience taught me to be wary of the "illustration." Often as preachers we feel obliged to draw the attention of our hearers by inserting an appropriate story or experience—and too often that is all they remember. If the story or experience is not inherently connected with our God story, then all our preparation is a waste of time.

That's why I prefer to talk about incarnating the gospel. We can do that through our use of language that invites and makes real; we can do it through retelling the Bible story; we can do it through drawing explicit connections between the text and our lives. But always the gospel remains primary.

~~~

Using Incarnational Language

- Read voraciously, so that you learn the many ways language works.

- Listen to people around you speaking, on the train, in shops, at the movies. Follow the speech patterns of locals, and explore how different groups use language. How do age, ethnicity, education, and social status shape our speech?
- Try to use language which is descriptive, using all five senses. How does it look, feel, smell? Use phrases that generate feeling, experience, and memory.
- Don't restrict this sort of language to your illustrations and examples—use it with the scriptural text. Imagine you are there; play with words, use your imagination.
- Begin small. Often a detailed description of one small aspect of a scene will invite people to imagine the rest, rather than you trying to cover everything.
- Read books on writing by well-known authors, such as Stephen King, *On Writing*; Anne Lamott, *Bird by Bird*; Annie Dillard, *Teaching a Stone to Talk*.

We as preachers need to be skilled at using language, to be aware both of its power and potential and of its limits. The best way that I know to do that is to immerse myself in it, and one way of doing that is to read: fiction, nonfiction, poetry; all can help to develop our sense of words and how they work. It need not be "great" literature; anything that captures our attention and imagination can feed our own use of words.

But language alone is not enough. No matter how well we use words, if the content of what we say is irrelevant, then so will be our words and, ultimately, our preaching. Incarnating the gospel means living—being incarnate—in this world of ours: Not for us is the ivory tower where we have leisure and independence to write; we need to be fully engaged with the gritty realities of everyday life, life where everything is interconnected and interdependent. And it's often not the broad sweep that matters so much as the detail: the grinding of air through a didgeridoo, the shoulder shaking and steadying, the smell of warm moist soil after a summer storm. These are the things that catch the attention of our hearers, that remind them of the authenticity of our shared life. That's why often the best preachers are not seminary professors but parish clergy, used to living and speaking in a gritty chaos wrenched open to the gaze of God.

~⁀

Finding and Speaking of God in the Everyday

- Pay attention. Where might God be found in the mall? In your back garden? In the group of kids hanging out on the coffee-house steps?
- Keep your eyes open. Often small details make the best illustration: the fall leaves beginning to turn color, the way bread crumbs when you cut it, what windows are in your church and what you can see in and through them.
- Look for the particular, the concrete, and describe it so that others can visualize it.
- Use real life, in such a way that people recognize themselves.
- Be careful that you are not betraying others' confidence—always ask permission.
- Be disciplined. If it's not quite right, don't use it.

~⁀

Every part of our lives feeds our preaching. If we have done our work of reading our text receptively and relationally, we can't help but carry it round with us and find connections in all sorts of unexpected places. We become experts at noticing where God may be at work, what Barbara Brown Taylor describes as being "detectives of divinity."[7] Our task then, is to bring these flashes of God to the ears and eyes and hearts of our hearers, in the hope that they too may learn to search out God at work in their own lives.

Sometimes we will end up with a traditional illustration. Sometimes we will speak of an experience. Sometimes we will use words to bring alive the story of God. But our touchstone is always God, the One in whom we hope and pray and whom we desire beyond all things to encounter, and who brings life to our lives. Embodied preaching means speaking what is in our bones, the things we know from a life lived immersed in the Holy, and inviting others to join us in that faith.

Right Beside Them
A Sermon

The people stood shivering in the knee-deep river, eyes gritty with the sandy desert dust, skin stinging from cold river water on blisters raised by the white-hot sun, mud slimy between their toes.

They had come to see a man, a prophet, some said he was, like that prophet in the old stories they had learned when they were just children, Elijah his name. They had come to see him, throwback to another century in his nomad's rough-woven clothes and belt torn from a dead animal's skin. They had come to see him on the strength of a rumor, out into this place of desolation—a wilderness of sudden precipices, thirst-quenching water dissolving to salt under your tongue, caves sheltering bears with honey-bronze coats shielding mauling claws, and the eerie scream of a mountain lion at night.

They had come to see him, to jeer and to mock, and had stayed to listen, his words curiously compelling in the strange desert silence, insinuating their way into their very guts. They had come to see him, and he had seen them, seen past their social smiles and ready laughter, past their city suits and business addresses, past even the calluses of work and the deep-etched lines of worry and blame, seen them in all the nakedness of their fear and doubt and shame, seen them, and baptized them. "Repent! Get ready for God!" is what he said.

And as they stood there with water trickling down their necks, I wonder what they were thinking. Did they wonder what they had gotten themselves into? Did they wonder if they had lost their minds? Did they wonder if it was someone's bizarre idea of a practical joke? What had they come to see?

Close to two thousand years later, the story of John the Baptist is as strange as ever. Walking into church at the beginning of December, the last thing I have on my mind is a desert preacher and his message of repentance. My mind is filled with other things: What on earth can I get my father this year? And when will I have time to go shopping? Where did I put the tree decorations? Who will I spend Christmas with? Will the snow make a mockery of all my plans? And over it all, around every corner I turn, constantly echoing in my mind, the carol's frenzied refrain: "Christmas is here, bringing good cheer, duh de-de duh, duh de-de duh. . . . Christmas is here, Christmas is here, Christmas is here."

Walking into church, I'm looking for a respite from the manic world outside, looking for a respite, a place of peace and quiet, to ponder the real meaning of Christmas.

Instead I get John the Baptist. A wild man standing in the desert, his voice stridently shouting, "Repent!"

The voice of John the Baptist is not a voice I particularly want to hear this first Sunday in December, and the penetrating eyes are not eyes I want to look into. Because they come with a message that I am just not ready to hear.

"Get ready," he says, with an urgency I rarely feel, except in the panic-stricken hours before the stores close on Christmas Eve, "get ready for God."

"Prepare the way of the Lord," John says, "make his paths straight." His voice echoes through the centuries, echoes to us, as he himself echoes the words of another prophet, the prophet Isaiah:

"In the wilderness prepare the way of the Lord, make straight in the desert a highway for our God. Every valley shall be lifted up, and every mountain and hill be made low; the uneven ground shall become level, and the rough places a plain. Then the glory of the Lord shall be revealed and all people shall see it together, for the mouth of the Lord has spoken."

If I were doing a children's talk, I would probably have in front of me a big box full of sand. I would have built a wonderful rugged landscape, with tall mountains, higher than the Rockies could ever hope to be, and deep gorges, the Grand Canyon repeated over and over again. Or even better, modeling clay, because then I could add color and detail—there would be precipices and black caves, jagged peaks and slopes of boulders and blue-green glaciers. And then, when the earth stood before me in all its glory, I would take a child's toy truck, a miniature bulldozer, and I would prepare the way of the Lord, cutting a highway through the landscape. The clay I dug out for tunnels would go to make bridges, and the cuttings from the sides of mountains would go to fill in valleys, and over it all I would roll a nice smooth strip of black clay, a highway for our God, who would then appear, presumably, in his miniature silver Mercedes, to drive along my beautiful road.

But is this what it's all about, is this what Isaiah, is this what John the Baptist really wanted us to hear? Is this what it means to prepare the way? You know, I don't think so. The voice in the wilderness might be crying, "Prepare the way of the Lord," but the way he is crying it is not just with words, but with a baptism of repentance and forgiveness. And why? Because God is coming. Because God is coming, and they'd better be ready. Because God is coming, and all that fear and doubt and shame, which John has seen in then, needs to be cleaned away, can be cleaned away, so that they will be ready for God.

But it's too late! For the next thing they know, God is there. They are still standing in the middle of that muddy river, wondering what on earth they have got themselves into, and God is there.

Right there beside them, knee deep in that muddy river with water trickling down his neck. Jesus joins them in their fear and doubt and shame, stands beside them in their brokenness.

This is the Word made flesh; the mouth of God has indeed spoken.

This Word made flesh, this God, came not in a silver Mercedes but on foot, this Word made flesh, this God, doesn't wait for everything to be cleaned up and made safe, but comes out into the place which is most dangerous and dark and threatening, comes and stands beside them, and offers them forgiveness.

Forgiveness, when the lumps and bumps inside of them could be smoothed, and the sharp points which tore every time they moved could be sanded round, and the bottomless empty valleys filled, and they could be healed and made whole.

Christmastime we sometimes think that everything has to be nice for God to come. A clean stable, the angels all in tune, our hearts prepared, to use the old clichés.

But it was a whole lot more messy than that when Christ came to the stable, a typical bloody, painful birth. It was a whole lot more messy when he came to the wilderness, a dangerous, desolate place. It was a whole lot more messy than that when he came to the cross, an excruciating, fearful death. The Word made flesh, come to stand with us.

So it seems to me that being ready for God isn't so much about getting everything cleaned up and perfect, but more about standing in the midst of the mess, in the midst of the unfinishedness of things, in the midst of danger and desolation, standing, and being honest about who we are and what we regret and fear and dream, learning to cry out to God from the depths of our being, "God, why did you let me catch a glimpse of the beauty of love, only to see the horror of love betrayed?" "Why did you give me these gifts only to find that no one wants them?" "God, why did you let me begin on this course, only to lose my way?" Standing in the midst of the mess, wondering why on earth we are here, and ready to see whatever answer God may give.

The answer is Jesus. The answer is Jesus, not like in Sunday School, when any five-year-old can work out that the answer is always Jesus, but the answer is . . . is in the Word made flesh, come to dwell among us, full of grace and truth.

In the places that seem impenetrable, in the fears and the uncertainties and the brokenness, Jesus comes. Right there in the wilderness, where it is most dangerous and threatening, Jesus comes. Right here and now, Jesus comes, offering forgiveness, and healing, and hope.

Standing shivering in the river, water trickling down their necks, praying for forgiveness and healing and hope, the people look up.

And there, right beside them, is the Christ.

December 5, 1999—Advent 2, Year B
Isaiah 40:1–11; Mark 1:1–8
St. John's Episcopal Cathedral, Denver, Colorado

What We Know
A Sermon

There are some things that I find terribly hard to believe.

I find it hard to believe that I won't fall out of the ride at an amusement park when it turns upside down.

I find it hard to believe that if I go over the edge of a cliff with a rope and a harness, I won't fall to my death.

I find it hard to believe that I could have fun if I stand on two thin planks of wood and slide down a steep hill covered with snow.

But in the end it doesn't really matter if I believe those things or not. Skiing and rock climbing and riding roller coasters are fun, but I can survive without them. Or I can give them a try, and see if believing comes any easier.

But there are other things we find it hard to believe that matter a lot. Other things which make a difference to the whole way we see the world. Other things which make a difference to whether we experience hope or despair.

Sometimes, we find it hard to believe the very things which make life livable.

Too often, we have heard in the last couple of weeks of the misery of kids who feel alienated, rejected by their peers, who find it hard to believe that anyone could love them. And so they cover it up and hide it away, they build protective walls to try to stop the hurt, and when that doesn't work, they do the one thing which from experience they do know how to do, and hurt others.

We have learned that violence isn't the answer. It doesn't help us believe the things we need to believe but can't. It doesn't fill that space that most of us feel at one time or another, when we feel most unloved: Whether it's because we feel like we are different, and just don't fit in. Whether we've done something awful, or perhaps just stupid. Whether we've listened too well to the voices which tell us that we can never be enough, never do enough, to be loved.

What caught my attention when first I read today's reading from Deuteronomy was just a few words hidden in the middle.

There we have a long recitation of all God has done for the people, kind of a summary of Genesis and Exodus. There's creation, God giving the breath of life to everything on this earth. There's Moses and the burning bush, there's the people's escape from Israel, and there's God speaking to the people now, in the middle of the wilderness.

And then there's these few words: "because God loved your ancestors, he chose their descendants after them." Because God loves your grandparents, and great-grandparents, and great-great grandparents before them, God chose you, and loves you too. All these stories, repeated time and time again to remind the people just how much God loves them.

We have our stories too. Stories which we add to those of the Old Testament stories of a God who loves us so much that in Christ he came to live among us, in Christ he died for us, in Christ he rose for us, so that we can live in the hope of life and love which will never end.

Christ who says, "Those who love me will be loved by my Father, and I will love them and reveal myself to them." Who says, "Love one another, as I have loved you."

We hear it so often, but we need to keep telling the stories, keep telling the stories, so that we can begin to believe that this is who God has always been, who God always is: One who loves us more than we can imagine, more than we can hope to believe. One who calls us to be loved, and to love. And keep telling the stories of how God has met us and loved us in our own lives, of how we share that love with each other.

A great chain of love going back as far as we can remember, and a long time before, which extends from God to us, and from us to one another.

"For the love of God is broader than the measure of the mind and the heart of the Eternal is most wonderfully kind."

A friend of mine, every night when he tucks his son in bed, says, "I love you, Josh." And Josh answers, "I love you too, Dad."

But one night, not so long ago, something was different. "I love you, Josh," he said. And Josh said, "I know that."

"I know that."

May we, too, know what it is sometimes hard to believe, that we are loved, that God loves us, passionately, from the very depth of God's being to the very depths of ours.

May 2, 1999—Evensong
Deuteronomy 4:32–40; John 14:15–20
Trinity Church, Princeton, New Jersey

NOTES

1. Julian of Norwich, *Showings*, trans. Edmund Colledge, OSA, and James Walsh, SJ (New York: Paulist Press, 1978), 186.

2. Jana Childers, *Performing the Word: Preaching as Theater* (Nashville, TN: Abingdon Press, 1998), 26.

3. Andrew Watterson Blackwood, *The Preparation of Sermons* (New York: Abingdon Press, 1948), 206–7.

4. Albert Mehrabian, *Silent Messages: Implicit Communication of Emotion and Attitudes* (Belmont, CA: Wadsworth Publishing, 1971), 43–44.

5. Psalm 29:4. *The Liturgical Psalter*, English text 1976, 1977; "inclusive language" version 1995, David L. Front, John A. Emerton, Andrew A. Macintosh (HarperCollins).

6. Two useful books on sermon delivery are Charles L. Bartow, *The Preaching Moment: A Guide to Sermon Delivery* (Dubuque, IA: Kendall/Hunt Publishing, 1995), and Childers, *Performing the Word*.

7. Barbara Brown Taylor, *The Preaching Life* (Cambridge, MA: Cowley Publications, 1993), 15.

About the Author

Raewynne J. Whiteley is rector of Saint James Episcopal Church in Saint James, New York. Born, raised, and ordained in Australia, she came to the United States for doctoral studies (in homiletics) and stayed. Preaching has been her passion since she took her first preaching class at the age of nineteen; she coedited *Get Up Off Your Knees: Preaching the U2 Catalog* (Cowley Publications, 2003). When not working, she enjoys hiking, knitting, kayaking, reading mystery novels, driving her Beetle, and spending time with her beloved cat, Bede.

18905064R00087

Made in the USA
Lexington, KY
28 November 2012